الكتاب المساعد

في

الكتابة

موافق لمستوى الشهادة العامة للتعليم الثانوي

جي سي أس إي أو ما يشابهها

The Writing Guide

Suitable for Arabic GCSE Course or Similar

Based on the EDEXCEL 2017 Specification

غسان نعمان ماهر

mm Books

الطبعة الجديدة 1439هـ/ 2018م

First published 2002
Second (expanded) edition 2002
Reprinted 2003
Third (expanded) edition 2008
Fourth (revised) edition 2011
New revised edition 2018

MM Books
PO Box 472
RUISLIP HA4 4JE, U.K.
Tel: 0044 7810 38 44 99
Email: mmbks@nildram.co.uk, sales@mmbooks.co.uk, info@mmbooks.co.uk

المـحـتوى

CONTENTS

القسم الأول   متطلبات الكتابة

القسم الثاني   الكتابة في المواضيع المختلفة

الملاحق

مقدمة الطبعة الجديدة 2017

Introduction to the new 2017 edition

This is the new edition of this unique and popular book, The Writing Guide *(it used to form part of The Grammar and Writing Guide, but is now split into two separate guides: this one and The Grammar and Translation Guide – GCSE 2017, please refer to the following link on our website https://www.mmbooks.co.uk/gcse-arabic-books-s/1821.htm)*, which was produced with two goals in mind: to enhance the teaching of writing practice, and to conform to the recent changes in the Arabic language Specification and assessment with Edexcel, one of the leading examination board in the United Kingdom. This revised edition should help teachers and students to immediately benefit from the book without making amendments and changes to make them suitable for the new Specification. However, in addition to the changes with regards to the topics and writing tasks, there is another major change in this edition:

the ruled pages that were intended for writing the writing exercises have been removed, simply because, if kept, the size of the book would expand excessively without great.

The writing test: description, marks

The GCSE Arabic writing test represents 25% of the examination. Most students find this test far more difficult than the reading and listening tests, and hence more marks are lost in this test. This is why this guide has been prepared.

The writing test – HIGHER TIER consists of three questions:

Question 1 (20 out of 60 marks) requires informal writing of 80-90 words, which, quoting the specification, 'assesses
students on their ability to convey information, narrate, express opinions, interest, and convince the reader about a certain point' (students select to answer one of two given options);

Question 2 (28 out of 60 marks) requires formal writing of 130-150 words, which, quoting the specification, 'assesses
students on their ability to convey information, narrate, express and justify ideas and opinions, and interest or convince the reader' (students select to answer one of two given options);

Question 3 (12 out of 60 marks) requires the translation of a short paragraph from English into Arabic.

A brief description of the requirements of each question is given on the first page of the chapter dealing with that question.

The questions are from all topics of the five themes of the specification.

This Guide aims to provide for the requirements that the specification and examinations expect from candidates in (a) topic-related content (b) elements of the candidate's response (i.e. description, opinion etc), and (c) grammar and other elements that relate to the structure and accuracy of the language.

Layout of the guide

This guide is divided into two parts: Part 1 for writing requirements, and Part 2 for written pieces that are suitable for the two GCSE writing questions. English is used extensively to ensure understanding by students.

The grammar element

In the GCSE writing paper, grammar will be tested in the writing questions. This includes the correct use of grammatical structures related to time (past, present and future) - and, needless to say, the correct use of fundamental grammar, such as prepositions, is necessary. This is provided (also in a revised, improved and a slightly expanded manner, in The Grammar and Translation Guide - GCSE 2017 mentioned above.)

Structures and other elements

Part 1 contains advice on punctuation, style and handwriting. The style section contains a list of many words which I call "connecting words", since they are used to connect the different parts of sentences or paragraphs to make the written pieces flow and give character to the writing; in addition to these are the 'fillers' that are used in informal speech (which is required for Question 2 of the GCSE writing paper.) Many may find the use of these, or some of them, too complex for this level, however, the Guide is expected to be used by students of different abilities and for different goals, many of whom will proceed to higher levels.

The elements of planning

During the course and in the examination, good planning before writing will always be beneficial. In Chapter 4, types of planning methods are given, with special emphasis on mind-maps. The author believes that this method is more useful than the others and, hence mind-maps are used in the written pieces in Part 2.

The written pieces in this book

The Guide contains ready-written pieces chosen according to the common topic areas for any course at this level; they are indeed general topics of writing. They match the latest Edexcel's Arabic Specification for the examinations in summer 2019 and thereafter. This includes providing for both informal and formal registers/speech style, separating them into two chapters - 5 and 6.

If students think that other topics are missing, this serves as an opportunity for them to practise writing and add more pieces to their repertoire. After all, writing in all areas and for all questions must be practised throughout the course, and this Guide should not be viewed as a book of ready-made pieces only. Before embarking on studying the pieces, you should read the introduction on the first page of each of the two writing chapters.

The pieces contain the following elements:
1- A sequential number (using 'INF' for informal-style tasks and 'FR' for formal-style tasks, to make it easier to identify for GCSE students):
   Question 1 (80-90 words) INF-1 to INF-27
   Question 2 (130-150 words) FR-1 to FR-28
2- A task, either a question or request
3- The task is in both languages, Arabic and English, (although the examination paper of the new GCSE specification uses Arabic only)
4- The pieces contain more words than the suggested/expected number of words for any particular task (it includes a variety of verbs, nouns, and descriptive and connecting words, so that students may use these according to their ability and style)
5- Some of the possibly difficult words are translated
6- The number of words is given so that the task of condensing a piece becomes easier, and also to help when writing similar pieces.

Index

At the back of the book, there is a quick-reference index to all the written pieces.

Vocabulary list

The vocabulary list has been removed in this new edition as it is now available, with full translations, for free download, in both Word format and pdf, from Edexcel's website.

However, <u>verb tables</u> have been added to this edition, which should help students to use the correct forms of the verbs for all pronouns: first, second and third person, in all tenses; past, present and the imperative.

Practice, practice and more practice!

Finally, nothing benefits more from practice than languages. You can learn to speak fluently - but not writing - by speaking with native speakers all the time. Practising writing, along with continuous reading, which provides more vocabulary and expressions, is essential for learning to write pieces that provide not only good communication but also pleasing style and composition.

To the teacher - a teaching perspective

Since the examination concerns writing, in its different forms and lengths and different fields of experience, preparing the student/candidate should aim to teach him or her not only to produce writing that can convey the ideas, but also writing which is as free as possible from grammatical, structural and handwriting errors. This level of language ability calls for a considerable amount of vocabulary and in its various meanings, as well as a good command of grammar, so preparation in its successive stages has to proceed with varying emphasis on the three disciplines: reading, grammar and writing. Hence, reading - along with vocabulary - will perhaps have the major emphasis at the beginning, with some handwriting training, and serious but not-so-fast coverage of grammar, trying to use newly acquired vocabulary in grammar exercises.

After the student has acquired a fair amount of vocabulary and reasonable command of grammar, writing long sentences, then paragraphs and short pieces can begin. Gradually, the student starts to write longer and more challenging pieces, all the time encouraged to find more ideas and details to fill longer pieces.

Improvement in structure will follow automatically from continued daily reading. Therefore, one cannot overemphasize the need for reading on daily basis, even for half an hour, or even fifteen minutes, but with much more during weekends and holidays.

The addition of a translation element in the new specification is expected to enhance and speedy up learning, because translation helps in acquiring a better understanding of grammar and expression, and more vocabulary, in addition to strengthening confidence in writing - in other words, there is a mutually beneficial relationship between translating and writing.

Important notice: HIGHER TIER only

For those using this book to prepare for GCSE examinations following the new 2017 Edexcel Specification, it is important to note that candidates can now sit their examinations in its FOUNDATION TIER or HIGHER TIER. The Foundation Tier can achieve 1 to 5 in the new 9-1 system, which corresponds to grades G to low B or high C in the old A*-G system, while the Higher Tier can achieve from 4 to 9 in the new system, which is C to A* in the old grading system. Since the majority of candidates and their teachers, tutors and schools wish, expect and work towards achieving A* to C, now 4 and above, this book has been produced for the HIGHER TIER ONLY. Any candidate for the Foundation Tier should consult the Specification to make sure of the requirements of the course, and hence of the examination papers.

القسم الأول

متطلبات الكتابة

PART ONE

Writing Requirements

Arabic Grammar and Translation   علامات الفصل

Punctuation marks are characters used to separate written text into parts that are connected with different degrees of association. Each one of these punctuation marks will, thus, separate the text in a certain way so as to emphasize the aim or clarify the content. The end effect of all this is to make the text easier to read and also more stylish.

Punctuation marks

The main punctuation marks which you should use are:

(1) نُقطة (.) **full stop** – used at the end of a sentence or to separate two or more sentences which are linked in some way within the same paragraph, or to end a paragraph.

Examples: وصلنا إلى المحطة المركزية. وبعد دقائق ركبنا القطار. ولولا السرعة لما ضاعت الحقيبة.

(2) فارزة/فاصِلة (،) **comma** – used to break up one sentence into two or more pieces which are closely linked either as a list of items or to emphasize or highlight a condition, exception etc, or to separate a non-restrictive clause (جملة إعتراضية) from a main clause.

Example: وصلنا إلى المحطة، وبعد دقائق ركبنا القطار. ولولا السرعة، التي تحركنا بها، لما ضاعت الحقيبة.

Note how we have connected the two sentences – which were separated with a full stop earlier – by a comma, since the text concerns the same incident. Note also how in the second sentence above, we specified which speed by using a separate non-restrictive clause.

(3) عَلامة سؤال/ استِفهام (؟) **question mark** – used instead of the full stop at the end of an interrogative sentence.

Examples: هل وصلتم إلى المحطة في الوقت المناسب؟ لماذا ضاعت الحقيبة؟

(4) علامة تَعَجُّب (!) **exclamation mark** – used instead of a full stop when the aim is to show surprise, astonishment, irony etc.

Examples: وصلتم في دقائق؟ هذا حقًا عجيب! ماذا؟ ضاعت الحقيبة؟!

Note the use of both question mark and exclamation mark above.

أكيد إن تذكرة القطار رخيصة. أليس سعرها عشرات الدنانير!

In this example, the use of an exclamation mark highlights an irony.

(5) علامة تَرقِيم (:) **colon** – used before a list, explanation, example or extended quotation.

Examples: إشتريت عدة أشياء: حقيبة وثوبان وحذاء.

هناك سبب لتلك النتيجة: لم يدرس ممدوح إلا في الأيام الأخيرة.

المجلات أنواعها كثيرة. مثلاً: مجلة المرأة، والطفل، والرياضة، والعلمية، والعامة وغيرها.

(6) علامتا الإقتِباس ((( ))) **quotation marks** – used to separate a quotation.

Example: قال سهيل للمدير ـ: ((أنت لست أبي حتى تعطيني هكذا أوامر.))، ولكنه اعتذر بعدها.

Note how a colon can be used to separate the quotation from the introduction, and how the brackets ensure that there is no confusion between the quotation and the rest of sentence.

(7) ( ) ( ) القَوْسان brackets - used for additional information which is not essential to the sentence.

Example: قبل عدة سنوات (في عام 2014 بالتحديد) سافرنا إلى السودان لزيارة الأهل.

Here, what is between brackets can be omitted without much affecting the sentence.

(8) (/) خط مائِل slash or oblique - used to separate the day, the month and the year when writing

dates, or when giving two alternatives.

Examples: 2019 /3/ 7 إلى صالحة التذكرة   2018 /1/ 15 الرسالة تاريخ.   شربت ثلاث/ أربع حبات من الدواء.

Importance
From the above examples, it is obvious that punctuation marks are important to create good structure in your writing: your ideas will become clearer for the reader, less important clauses are clearly separated from the main body of the sentence, and quotations are separated to indicate precisely the quoted words and to improve readability. Your expressions can be affected or improved by the use of some of these marks, such as the exclamation mark.

Final checking
You should make it a habit to go back and read through what you have written to check that your punctuation are sufficient and correctly used, and if the whole of the written piece is quite readable.

Examples of incorrect/insufficient and corrected/sufficient punctuation

(1) ضغطت على زر الطابعة طابعتي الجديدة ولكنها لم تعمل، يبدو أن الكهرباء تركتنا مرة أخرى.

ضغطت على زر الطابعة (طابعتي الجديدة) ولكنها لم تعمل. يبدو أن الكهرباء تركتنا مرة أخرى!

(2) قال لي المعلم "أين نتائج التجربة". أجبته بأني لم أنته بعد. لكنه لم يصدقني إلا بعد الإلحاح، هل هذا معقول.

قال لي المعلم: ((أين نتائج التجربة؟)). أجبته بأني لم أنته بعد، لكنه لم يصدقني إلا بعد الإلحاح. هل هذا معقول؟!

(3) حوّلني الطبيب إلى المستشفى وهي مستشفى محلية، لعمل فحص الأشعة وهذه ثالث مرة أذهب إلى هناك.

حوّلني الطبيب إلى المستشفى (وهي مستشفى محلية)، لعمل فحص الأشعة، وهذه ثالث مرة أذهب إلى هناك.

(4) زرت عدة بلدان، مصر وتركيا واليمن وفرنسا. ولو أن سفرة مصر كانت الأفضل ومن نواحٍ عديدة.

زرت عدة بلدان: مصر وتركيا واليمن وفرنسا؛ ولو أن سفرة مصر كانت الأفضل، ومن نواحٍ عديدة.

(5) عجيب أمرك يا خالد تريد مساعدة إخواننا الفلسطينيين بمجرد الكلام ومشاهدة الأخبار، ما فائدة ذلك لهم؟

عجيب أمرك يا خالد! تريد مساعدة إخواننا الفلسطينيين بمجرد الكلام ومشاهدة الأخبار. ما فائدة ذلك لهم؟!

Chapter Two   الفصل الثاني

Style   الأسلوب

Generally, each person has his own way of writing which can reflect his personality, likes and dislikes, ambitions and inclinations. It is in your interest to have a personal style of writing, especially if it makes what you write pleasing to read. That said, you can always borrow phrases from famous sayings or lines of poetry to emphasize your ideas and to bring variety of expression to your writing.

Importance in the examination

If you are sitting the GCSE writing examinations, your style comes into play in both writing questions. Although in both writing questions, part of the marks is awarded for clear, relevant, unambiguous and coherent writing, and the other part to variety of vocabulary and structures, and how sentences – long, complex etc – are presented, as well as interest and variety or elegance of expression, examiners are looking for more when they mark question 2. In addition, accuracy in language and spelling has marks allocated to it in question 2 only. This, in addition to requiring a greater number of words to be written, is why more marks are allocated for question 2 than for question 1.

How

1- The way ideas are expressed – You should use narrative, description or direct reporting. More than one of these can be used together in one piece of writing. For example, you may be telling a story of an accident in your school and use narrative but with quotations from people involved, highlighting particular places by interesting description.

2- Structure of the whole piece – You should:

(a) Break the piece into paragraphs as appropriate;

(b) Use appropriate and effective punctuation;

(c) Try to make your piece flow. This last point calls for connecting paragraphs and sentences with appropriate connecting words. These words, not only clarify or emphasize the meaning, they also make the piece flow nicely and prevent it from appearing as broken strings of sentences similar to internet messages. In the next few pages, many of these connecting words are listed, along with their English meanings and examples. Following that is an attempt to show how these words can make what you write more interesting, by comparing four pairs of pieces.

(d) The use of 'fillers' is a feature of informal writing, which is the style required for question 1, if sitting the GCSE examinations. A list of 'fillers' follows the connecting words, with examples.

━━━━━ CHECKLIST ━━━━━

Try getting into the habit of checking that you have attended to all the requirements by using a suitable checklist. Such checklist can look like this:

1- Does my writing **fulfil the task**? (THIS IS FUNDAMENTAL.)

2- Did I use **a variety of tools of expression**? Did I use these effectively?

3- **Grammar**, especially checking the main items such as the *fatha nunation* (غدًا); or the

use of *alif* (أ), *ya'* (ي) or *wow* (و) in subject (فاعل), object (مفعول به), nouns after prepositions (الاسم المجرور), *mubtada'* and *khabar* (المبتدأ والخبر), *kana* and its sisters (كان وأخواتها), *inna* and its sisters (إن وأخواتها), pronouns (الضمائر) etc.

4- Is my **punctuation**, correct, effective, sufficient?

5- Is my piece **pleasing to read**? (Pleasing does not necessary mean making the reader joyful or happy. You may be writing about a tragic event, or your writing may be quite depressing, but still pleasing to read because it fulfils the task and engages the reader.)

الكلماتُ الرابطةُ   connecting words

(1) كذلِكَ ، أيْضًا : also / as well (كان معنا حقائب كثيرة، أكياس ملابس أيضًا، وكاميرات كذلك.)

كَما : also / as well (كان معنا حقائب كثيرة، كما كان هناك عدة كاميرات.)

بِالإِضافَةِ إِلى ذلِكَ : in addition / in addition to this (الغرف واسعة، بالإضافة إلى ذلك الطعام لذيذ.)

(Note that any one of the above words can be used instead of any of the others.)

(2) عادَةً : usually (عادة، أخرج من البيت الساعة الثامنة والنصف.)

إِعْتِيادِيًّا : normally (إعتياديًا، أزور طبيب الأسنان مرة كل ستة أشهر.)

غالِباً ما، في أَغلَبِ الأَحيان (الأَوْقات) : often / in most occasions (غالبًا ما ألعب في النادي.)

أَحيانًا، في بَعضِ الأَحيان : sometimes (لا أحب الخروج يوم السبت، ولكن أحيانًا أذهب إلى المسبح.)

(Note that the second part of the last sentence does not need to be used to make exceptions etc. أَحيانًا *can, for example, be used instead of* غالِباً ما *in the first sentence.)*

(3) إِلّا أَنَّ ، وَلكِنَّ : but (كانت الحفلة رائعة، إلا أن/ ولكن المدعوين كانوا قليلين.)

بِالرَّغْمِ مِن ، عَلَى الرَّغْمِ مِن : in spite of (بالرغم من/ على الرغم من أن المدعوين كانوا قلائل، فقد كانت الحفلة ناجحة.) أو (كانت الحفلة ناجحة بالرغم من/ على الرغم من أن المدعوين كانوا قلائل.)

مَعَ ذلِكَ : even though / nonetheless (المدعوون قلائل، مع ذلك كانت الحفلة ناجحة.)

(4) إِنَّما : it is (he is / she is / they are / you are / I am / we are) only (أخذت أشجع نفسي قائلاً: إنما هي قفزة واحدة.) (لم يبق شيء، إنما هو أسبوع واحد وتنتهي الامتحانات.)

(5) أَوْ : or *(e.g. Take this pen or that, but not both.)* (خُذ هذا القلم أو ذاك، ولكن لا تأخذ الإثنين.)

أَمْ : or *(e.g. I don't know whether to speak or not. /// Who has come: Ali or Karim?)*

(لا أدري هل أتكلم أَمْ لا.)   (من جاء: عليّ أَمْ كريم؟)

إِمّا ... أَوْ : either ... or (نسافر إما إلى تونس أَوْ مصر.) (ندخل إما إلى الفيلم أَوْ المسرحية.)

(6) لِذا ، لِذَلِكَ : consequently   (ظل عمي يدخن ثلاثين سنة، لِذلك أصيب بالسرطان!)

(7) إِذًا (إِذَنْ) : therefore   (لم نقطع تذكرة القطار، إِذًا علينا أن نذهب بالباص.)

(8) حَيْثُ : where / wherein / in which   (كان البحر رائعًا، حيث الشمس طالعة والشاطئ نظيف.)

حَيْثُ أَنّ : in view of the fact that / due to the fact that / since / because (حيثُ أَنّ الشقة لم تكن في الشارع الرئيسي، عليك أن تخفض السعر.) (حيث أن البرنامج قد تأخر لم لا نخرج نتمشى قليلاً؟)

بِحَيْثُ : to the extent that (كان العمل متواصلاً بحيث نسيت الغداء!) (تدربت يوميًا بحيث صرتُ خبيرًا.)

(9) فِي حِين : whereas (خسر جمال في حين فاز فاروق.) (شفيتُ في يومين في حين بقيتَ أنت على حالك.)

(10) حَتَّى : until (e.g. We waited until the afternoon.) (إنتظرنا حتى العصر.) (مشينا حتى آخر الشارع.)

حَتَّى : even (e.g. Everyone came even the neighbours.)   (جاء الجميع حتى الجيران.)

حَتَّى وَلا ، وَلا حَتَّى : not even (e.g. No one came, not even him.) (لم أشترِ ولا حتى/ حتى ولا جوارب.)

(11) أَعلاهُ ، في أَعلاهُ : above (إرجع إلى الجملة أعلاه/ في أعلاه.) (صعدت البيت ونظرت أعلاه.)

أَدناهُ ، في أَدناهُ : below (حلّ التمرين أدناه/ في أدناه.) (أصاب الطين سروالي في أدناه.)

فِيما سَيأْتِي ، فيما يَلِي : hereunder / what will come (أنظر الحلّ فيما يلي.) (الخير فيما سيأتي.)

(12) مَثَلاً ، مِثل : such as   (زرنا الكثير من الأماكن، مثلاً/ مثل قصر العظم والجامع الأموي.)

مِثال عَلَى ذَلِكَ : as an example of that (العرب كرماء، مثال على ذلك الاستقبال الحسن في المغرب.)

(13) لا شَكَّ في : no doubt, undoubtedly / without doubt (لا شك في أن المخدرات تدمر الصحة وتغضب الله.)

(14) أَبَدًا : at all   (لم أستطع الكلام أبدًا فقد كان المنظر مخيفًا.) (لا تتكلم مع أمك باستهزاء أبدًا.)

(15) بِالطَّبْعُ : obviously / naturally (بالطبع اشتريت هدايا تذكارية.) (بالطبع ليس كل كتاب مفيد.)

(16) أَمّا : as for/regarding/as far as... is (are/was/were) concerned

(أما السيارة فقد صلحت، وأما التلفاز فلا .)

(17) بَلْ : rather (المباراة كانت بطيئة، بل كانت مملة!) (وصلنا مطار جدة في الليل، بل عند الفجر .)

(18) نَعَم ، بَلى : yes (نعم/ بلى، لقد قضينا وقتًا طيبًا هناك .)

مُؤَكَّد ، أَكِيد : certainly / indeed (مؤكد/ أكيد أن الأخبار صحيحة.) (كان الخبر مؤكدًا/ أكيدًا .)

لا ، كَلاّ : no (لا/ كلا، لم أدخل في شبكة الأنترنت أمس.) (لا/ كلا، القميص أبيض وليس أسود.)

رُبَّمَا : maybe / perhaps (ربما وصلنا إلى المكان المطلوب.) (ربما يكون الحاسوب عاطلاً.)

قَدْ : certainly / something did happen (قد جاء الشتاء.) (نعم، لقد تم إرسال الفاكس.)

عَلَى الأَكْثَر : at most (على الأكثر سنبيت الليلة في الفندق.) (لم يأت لأنه على الأكثر مشغول.)

(19) بِعِبَارَةٍ أُخرَى : in other words (الجار على اليمين يسمع الراديو عاليًا، والذي على اليسار يتشاجر مع أولاده كل يوم، أما الذي أمامنا فكلبه يعوي باستمرار؛ بعبارة أخرى، نحن نعيش في جحيم!)

(20) لا سِيَّمَا : especially (العروس جميلة، لا سيما شعرها.) (أحب درس التاريخ، لا سيما الحديث.)

(21) بِمَا أَنَّ : as / because (بما أنك لم تحضر، لن تشارك.) (بما أن الناس ملابسهم خفيفة، إذًا الجو حار.)

(22) عَلَى أَيِّ (أَيَّةِ) حَال : at any rate / any way (المرض ووفاة جدك والانتقال إلى دار أخرى كلها أمور تؤثر على الدراسة. ولكن على أي حال، عليك دخول الامتحان بثقة.)

(23) يَبْدُو أَنَّ ، يَظْهَر أَنَّ : it seems that (يبدو أن/ يظهر أن المصرف مغلق.) (يبدو أنه/ يظهر أنه مغلق.)

(24) عَدا، فِيمَا عَدا ، ما عَدا ، بِاسْتِثناء ، سِوَى : except / save (عدا/ فيما عدا/ ما عدا/ باستثناء مراد، علاقتي ممتازة مع الجميع.) (علاقتي ممتازة مع الجميع سوى/ عدا/ فيما عدا/ ما عدا/ باستثناء مع مراد.)

(Note the use of all words except سوى which we would not normally use at the beginning of speech.)

(25) لا بُدَّ من : it is a must (لا بد من التلقيح قبل السفر.) (على الرغم من المصاعب، لا بد من الذهاب.)

(26) بِمُجَرَّدِ أَنْ ، ما أَنْ : as soon as (بمجرد أن/ ما أن وصلنا، أكلنا.) (أكلنا بمجرد أن/ ما إن وصلنا.)

(27) عِبَارَة عَنْ : is (are / was / were) / tantamount to (هذا الجهاز عبارة عن طابعة صغيرة.) (كانت التجربة عبارة عن استعمال مقياس الحرارة.)

(28) عِندَما : as/when   (عندما كنتُ أحضّر حقيبتي ألغي السفر.)

(29) في حال : in case   (خذ الأدوات معك فإنها تنفع في حال عطل السيارة.)

(30) وَلا : neither   (لم يذهبوا إلى النادي ولا أنا.)

لا ... وَلا : neither ... nor   (التدخين غير مسموح لا ولا تناول الطعام.)

(31) وإلاَّ/ بِعَكْسِهِ : otherwise   (أدرس جيداً، وإلا/ بعكسه لن تؤدي الامتحان كما ينبغي.)

(32) إلاَّ إذا : unless   (لن أشترك إلا إذا اشتركتما معي.)

(33) وفْقاً لـ/ طِبْقاً لـ : according to (وفقاً للتقرير/ طبقاً للتقرير، يوجد عجز في الميزانية.)

(34) لأنّ/ بِسَبَب : because   (بسبب الإهمال/ لأنه مهمل لم ينجح في الامتحان.)

(35) لكِنْ/ لكِنَّ : but   (لم يأت لكنْ أرسل اعتذاراً.) (لم يأت لكنّه أرسل اعتذاراً.)

(36) حَتّى وَلَوْ : even if   (لا ينفعني حتى ولو جعلها مضاعفاً.)

(37) وَمَعَ ذلِك : however   (رفضت الذهاب، ومع ذلك أبقيت الباب مفتوحاً للحل.)

(38) إذا : if   (إذا وصلت في الموعد يمكن أن نذهب سويةً.) (لا يمكن القبول إذا بقي معانداً.)

(39) لِكَيْ/ لأجْل : in order to   (ذهبت معه لكي أشجعه.) (ذهبت معه لأجل تشجيعه/ أن أشجعه.)

(40) ثُمَّ : then   (وصل نادر ثم إياد.) (الدراسة الدقيقة أولاً ثم المراجعة السريعة.)

(41) لِذلكَ/ وبِناءً عَلَيْه : therefore   (تأخروا كثيراً، لذلك سألغي الموعد.) (النتائج واضحة، وبناء عليه سنتقدم بالاقتراحات اللازمة.)

(42) أوَّلاً وقَبْلَ كُلِّ شيءٍ : first of all (أولاً وقبل كل شيء عليك أن تعتذر إليه.)

(43) أخيراً : finally   (أخيراً، وصلنا إلى نهاية الكتاب.)

Now compare...

Now let's see how using these words can improve what you write by comparing the following pairs of pieces. Each piece is taken from a longer piece and is written twice. Although the first version is quite acceptable, the second version has benefited from some of the above words. This is underlined. Read the first piece aloud, then the second, improved version, and you will notice the difference immediately.

(1) رسالة – شاب من هواة المراسلة يتعرف على شاب آخر   letter

• أخبرك أني أحب التعرف على جميع بلدان الوطن العربي. لا مانع من أن أستَضِيفَك هنا في العطلة الصيفية أو الشتوية. سأكون مسرورًا لو تمكّنت من زيارة بلدكم والتعرف عليه عن قُرب.

عمري 16 سنة وفي المرحلة الثانوية. والدي يعمل معلّمًا وأمي تعمل موظفة في بنك. عندي أخ وأخت أصغر منّي.

هواياتي هي كرة القدم والتصوير وكتابة الشعر... ستقول أنها هوايات لا تجتمع في شخص واحد! أمي تقول أني لا أشبه الآخرين في أي شيء. وأظن أنها صادقة.

أرفق صورة لي، وبعض الصور التي صورتها لمنطقتنا والتي فازت إحداها بجائزة المدرسة.

• أخبرك أني <u>أولاً وقبل كل شيء</u> أحب التعرف على جميع بلدان الوطن العربي، وليس <u>عندي أي</u> مانع من أن أستَضِيفَك هنا في العطلة الصيفية أو الشتوية. <u>كما</u> سأكون مسرورًا لو تمكّنت من زيارة بلدكم والتعرف عليه عن قُرب.

أوه... نسيت بسبب حَماسي الشديد أن أخبرك أن عمري 16 سنة <u>وأني</u> في المرحلة الثانوية. والدي يعمل معلّمًا وأمي تعمل موظفة في بنك (<u>مصرف</u>). عندي أخ وأخت، <u>كلاهما</u> أصغر منّي.

هواياتي هي كرة القدم (<u>طبعًا!</u>) والتصوير وكتابة الشعر... <u>ربما</u> ستقول أنها هوايات لا تجتمع في شخص واحد! <u>على أي حال</u> أمي تقول أني لا أشبه الآخرين في أي شيء! وأظن أنها صادقة!

<u>أخيراً</u>، أرفق صورة لي، وبعض الصور (<u>وهي مُصَغَّرة</u>) التي صورتها لمنطقتنا والتي فازت إحداها بجائزة المدرسة.

(2) محادثة – مقارنة الجو في بلدين عربيين وبريطانيا   conversation

• مصطفى: كيف كان الجو في سورية عندما زرتها في عطلة أعياد الميلاد يا ياسين؟

ياسين: لن تُصدّق! في بعض الأيام كنت أظن أنني لا زِلت في انجلترا!

مصطفى: ماذا؟ يعني أن الجو كان باردًا...

ياسين: باردًا؟! هذه كلمة خفيفة جدًا! الثلج نزل ونزلت الحرارة إلى تحت الصفر!

مصطفى: صحيح؟ لم أكن أعرف أن ذلك ممكن الحدوث في بلد عربي.

ياسين: ظهر أن هذا يحدث كثيرًا، والشتاء بارد كل سنة. والأمطار قليلة جدًا بالقياس إلى انجلترا.

مصطفى: ولكن الجو لم يكن باردًا في القاهرة، ولا في الاسكندرية؟

• مصطفى: كيف كان الجو في سورية عندما زرتها في عطلة أعياد الميلاد يا ياسين؟

ياسين: مؤكد أنك لن تُصدّق! أحيانًا كنت أظن أنني لا زِلت في انجلترا!

مصطفى: ماذا؟ لا بد أن الجو كان باردًا...

ياسين (مقاطعًا): باردًا؟! هذه كلمة خفيفة جدًا! لقد نزل الثلج ونزلت الحرارة إلى تحت الصفر!

مصطفى: صحيح؟ لم أكن أعرف أن ذلك ممكن الحدوث في بلد عربي.

ياسين: بل ظهر أن هذا يحدث كثيرًا، كما أن الشتاء بارد كل سنة. إلاّ أنّ الأمطار قليلة جدًا بالقياس إلى انجلترا.

مصطفى: ولكن الجو لم يكن باردًا في القاهرة، حتى ولا في الاسكندرية (التي على البحر)؟

report   (3) تقرير – العمل في العطلات

• العمل في العطلات متنوع ويكون مُمتِعًا. فالعمل في المتاجر والتعرف على الناس. وفي النّوادِي الرياضية والاجتماعية في أجواء بَهِيجة، أو يكون في المزارع لِجَنْي الفاكهة (والأكل منها!)، أو في المطاعم (مع الأكل أيضًا) أو في المكتبات فتكون ممتعة جدًا لمن يحب القراءة.

• العمل في العطلات متنوع، وقد يكون مُمتِعًا. ربما يكون العمل في المتاجر والتعرف على الناس (وشراء الملابس بتَخْفِيضات كبيرة!)، أو في النّوادِي الرياضية والاجتماعية في أجواء بَهِيجة، في حين يكون في المزارع لِجَنْي الفاكهة (والأكل منها طبعًا!)، أو في المطاعم (مع الأكل أيضًا، ولكن ليس سن فَضَلات الزبائن!)، أما في المكتبات فتكون لا شك ممتعة جدًا لا سيما لمن يحب القراءة ولذلك أفضّلها على غيرها حتى ولو أحصل على أجر أقل.

narrative   (4) قصة – سكن غير مريح في فندق

• صَعِدوا إلى الشُّقَّة فوجدوا الأثاث مقبولاً، ورائحة الحمام كانت كَرِيهَة، ولم يكن هناك ماء في الحَنَفِيَّة (الصّنْبور)! كان المطبخ الصغير وَسِخًا وأسلاك الطباخ ظاهِرَة للعَيان فخافوا من استعماله. فتح رياض سِتارَة الشباك

وصاح بدَهْشَة فأسْرَعَت سعاد وسامح الصغير إلى الشباك فرأوا مَوقِعًا للبناء خَلف الفندق والعمال والسيارات في عمل دَؤوب وسط الغُبار المُتصاعِد! يعني أنها لم تكن سفرة سياحة ولكن جولة في عالم البناء.

• صَعدوا إلى الشُقّة فوجدوا الأثاث مقبولاً، إلا أن رائحة الحمام كانت كَرِيهَة، كما لم يكن هناك ماء في الحَنَفِيَّة (الصّنْبور)! أما المطبخ الصغير فكان وَسِخًا وأسلاك الطباخ ظاهِرَة للعَيان بحيث خافوا من استعماله. بمجرد أن فتح رِياض سِتارَة الشباك صاح بدَهْشَة: ((ما هذا؟))، أسْرَعَت سعاد وسامح الصغير إلى الشباك فرأوا المنظر خلف الفندق عبارة عن مَوقِع للبناء والعمال والسيارات في عمل دَؤوب وسط الغُبار المُتصاعِد! بعبارة أخرى، لم تكن سفرة سياحية، وإنما جولة في عالم البناء!

كَلِماتُ الحَشْو   fillers

كلمات الحشو يمكن استخدامها في الكتابة "غير الرسمية" (informal)، بالإضافة إلى كلمات الربط أعلاه.

1) تدري / تعرف (أنت تدري/ تعرف/ تعلم) : you know   (تدري/ تعرف كان هناك مشروع معه.)

2) هو/ هي مثل : it's like   (هو هذا الموقف مثل الأسبوع الماضي.) (هي كلامها مثل كلام سوسن.)

3) زين / طيّب (لا بأس/ موافق) : ok   (طيّب، نذهب اليوم مساء.)

4) صحيح / نعم : right/true   (صحيح/ نعم جاء في الموعد، لكنه لم يكن جاهزاً للموضوع.)

5) بالحقيقة / في الحقيقة : actually   (لم يكن الامتحان سهلاً، بالحقيقة/ في الحقيقة كان صعباً جداً.)

6) ببساطة : simply   (ببساطة، لا يقبلون بأي اقتراح.)

7) أساساً/ في الأساس : basically   (هم أساساً رفضوا الطلب.) (في الأساس، لم يحصلوا عليه.)

8) لذلك/ وعليهِ : so   (صارت السفرة أسبوعاً كاملاً، لذلك/ وعليه زاد رسم الاشتراك 20%.)

9) زين / طيّب / إذاً : well   (لا تقبل بأي اقتراح، زين/ طيب/ إذاً إبحث عن شخص آخر.)

10) أقصد/ قصدي (ما أقصده/ ما أعنيه) : I mean   (لا لا، أقصد/ قصدي أن تنتظري ثم تكلمي معهم.)

Handwriting الخطّ

Importance

Handwriting is the vehicle by which you submit your thoughts, ideas, suggestions, responses, replies and the rest of your interaction with the outside world. It is, therefore, vital that it doesn't fall below the least acceptable level of being easy to read (and looks nice, why not?)

This becomes essential when it comes to your handwriting in an examination paper, for if the examiner is unable to decipher your handwriting, you cannot expect him to award you the marks you deserve. Legible handwriting is essential in any examination, otherwise marks are unnecessarily lost. Clear handwriting can be achieved by:

(a) writing the letters in a readable way

(b) using a small size and well separated words, rather than a large size and words crammed together.

How to improve your handwriting

Improving handwriting takes time because it requires practice. You must not delay this. Arabic calligraphy books prepared for students may be useful, but do not assume that these are meant for very young children; after all, your younger brother or sister might have a better handwriting than you! These books have the words and sentences written in proper calligraphy and also they gradually get more difficult. Moreover, they are ruled to help writing in horizontal, equally-separated lines.

Try to write slowly at first, paying attention to your handwriting. Gradually, as you build up your speed, you should find that you are writing not only quicker, but producing better handwriting.

Tidiness

Following illegibility, nothing puts off a reader more than messy and irregularly written pieces. Ensure that you use wide enough margins and line separations (although these should be already provided in the examination paper). To avoid messy areas due to omissions and additions, you should plan your piece carefully, perhaps as suggested in the coming pages.

Writing the *hamzah*   كيفية كتابة الهمزة

In addition to a few other letters where some people err when writing in Arabic, the *hamzah* stands out as the most problematic, since it can be written in four ways depending on the grammar of the word in which it forms part.

Here are the four possible ways of writing the *hamzah*, with explanations:

تكتب الهمزة حسب الحركة على الهمزة وحسب الحركة على الحرف الذي يسبق الهمزة.

أولاً : الهمزة على الألف – أ – 1 – إذا كانت الهمزة مفتوحة (عليها حركة الفتحة) مثل : أَنْ ، بِأَي

2 – إذا كان الحرف قبل الهمزة مفتوحًا مثل : يقرَأ ، نَبَأ

ملاحظة : يمكن استعمال المدّ (آ) بدلاً من الهمزة في حالة الفتح إذا جاء بعدها ألف مثل : يَقرَآن ، بدلاً من يقرَأان ، لكي لا نكرر كتابة الألف مرتين.

ثانيًا : الهمزة على الكرسي – ئـ أو ئ – 1 – إذا كانت الهمزة مكسورة (عليها حركة الكسرة) مثل : إنَّ ، سُئِلَ

2 – إذا كان الحرف قبل الهمزة مكسورًا مثل : نُبِّئْتُ ، نُبِّئَ

3 – إذا كان قبل الهمزة ياء (ي) ولم تكن الهمزة آخر الكلمة مثل : شَيْئًا ، رَدِيئان

ثالثًا : الهمزة على الواو – ؤ – 1 – إذا كانت الهمزة مضمومة (عليها حركة الضمة) مثل : رَؤُوف ، رَؤُفْت ، يُنَبَّؤُون

2 – إذا كان الحرف قبل الهمزة مضمومًا مثل : فُؤاد ، شُؤُون ، سُـؤال

رابعًا : الهمزة لوحدها – ء – 1 – إذا كان الحرف قبل الهمزة مسكَّنًا (عليه حركة السكون) مثل : شَيْء ، رِزْء ، سُـوء

2 – إذا كان قبل الهمزة ألف (ا) مثل : أسماء ، أنبـاء

ملاحظة : الفرق بين (شَيْء) و (نُبِّئ) أنه في الأولى كان الحرف قبل الهمزة (ي) مسكَّنة ، ولذلك كتبنا الهمزة بعدها لوحدها (ء) ، في حين أنه في الثانية كان الحرف قبل الهمزة مكسورًا ولذلك كتبنا الهمزة على الكرسي (ئ).

Planning Your Writing   التحضير للكتابة

When attempting any writing task, some people start directly without even a pause for thinking. The consequence of such a haphazard approach is that ideas are missed out, clarity is not achieved and messy pieces are produced because of additions and omissions. In an examination, this can never do you any good, and can indeed cost you valuable marks. Hence, planning is essential if you want to avoid such shortcomings and achieve higher grades.

Planning methods

For tackling questions or problems, people have devised many planning methods. No one can say that a particular method is better than another, for questions differ in their requirements and people differ in the way they think and present their solutions. For our purposes, we can look at several planning methods.

1- Thinking only

This is perhaps the most widely used method. Unfortunately, it is quite risky! All the above mentioned problems are associated with it. For even if you do stop to ponder before writing your piece, ideas may still be missed out, vagueness replaces clear thinking, and the paper ends up with many omissions and asterisks indicating additions at the bottom of the page - very irritating for the reader and examiner. This method may be used when the task is quite short. For longer pieces, however, you should try something more elaborate.

2- List of points

Listing the ideas that are suitable for the requirements of the question, in short points, is a good technique. This method not only makes it easier for you to follow later when you are writing, and safer too in ensuring that no ideas are missed out, but it also gives your mind a little more time to collect ideas while you are jotting down the list. However, the problem with lists is that they are sometimes too brief: they do not allow you to add sub-ideas, and may even prevent such sub-ideas from surfacing. For example, a list written for a story of a trip may include the following:

which holiday, how long   /   country, why   /   people in the trip   /

train, bus, ship or plane   /   in that country, visits, trips, shopping   /   conclusion

As you see, the list does not include how much will be written for each point. Also, there are no details about the most important part, which is the time spent inside the country you visited. Unless you are very lucky, the piece is bound to suffer from some, if not all, of the shortcomings of the 'thinking-only' approach.

3- List of paragraphs

This is similar to the above method, except that you make it clear from the outset the number of paragraphs and the content of each. This should help in writing the required number of words, and prevent you from going too much beyond that limit.

4- Mind-maps

Mind-maps, or spider diagrams as they are also called, are - as we shall see - the best method of planning your writing pieces. They use the radial approach, i.e. from the centre outwards. It is claimed by its proponents that this is the way in which our minds work and keep their information archives, and it is also the way in which nature is designed, down to the atom with its central nucleus and surrounding electron orbits.

Benefits of mind-maps

Many benefits can be derived from drawing a mind-map - as a summary:

1- great reduction of the size of the original text;

2- keeps an information hierarchy, thus preserving the degree of importance of each part;

3- clarity of the highest degree, since all the information is laid out on one sheet of paper;

4- excellent learning tool, because when constructing the mind-map you need to search thoroughly in the text you are working on for the pieces of information which need to be written and how to link them in a hierarchal way; this takes your learning to a much higher degree of concentration and, consequently, understanding;

5- a powerful tool for memorizing and revision, since it takes only few minutes to revise such a condensed summary;

6- for the writing pieces in question, mind-maps provide better planning than lists for two reasons:

   a- points, ideas or paragraphs are laid out in a clearer way (3 above);

   b- you can write down all the details of each idea, point or paragraph using the branches and sub-branches of the mind-map; this can provide you with almost the complete piece before starting.

Apart from our purposes here, I recommend that you use mind-maps throughout studying, as it is a powerful tool for learning, revising and answering in examinations. And what is more, if you have time to use diagrams, signs and colour, mind-maps can be great fun!

Examples of mind-maps

It should take only few minutes to plan your writing piece for question 1, or even for question 2. This very short time will be well-spent when you end up with a piece containing all your ideas or points, laid out in the order you want and neat and tidy. Avoiding unnecessarily long pauses to formulate an idea while you are writing, and avoiding having to add a sentence here and omit a sentence there, should provide you with valuable extra time at the end to attend to your checklist of question requirements, punctuation, grammar and style. In other words, using mind-mapping to plan your writing pieces should be timesaving as well.

The **method** is simple:

   1- Draw a circle in the centre of the area to be used and write the name of the task inside.
   2- Draw a branch from the circle and write the name of the point, detail etc alongside it.
   3- Draw branches from that branch and write in the details of that branch.
   4- Repeat with another main branch and sub-branches.
   5- If applicable, draw link lines or arrows between the various branches.
   6- Enter branch numbers according to the sequence in which you would like them to appear.

The mind-map can be drawn at the bottom or any spare space in your examination paper. It need not take up a large area or be very elaborate; after all, you have only few minutes to complete it.

Now, let's try using mind-mapping for writing pieces. These mind-maps have been produced using a computer program. You do not need that, either in the examination or if you use mind-maps in learning, summarizing and revising: mind-maps constructed by hand are just as good.

سؤال 1 – أكتب، في **80–90** كلمة، إلى أهلك من البلد العربي الذي تقضي فيه العطلة.

Question 1 - Write, in 80-90 words, to your family from an Arab country you are visiting.

In the following mind-map, constructed in English, see how the whole piece is now in front of you and how each branch represents a separate point. Note how it does not seem confusing even if the sequence of branches does not follow the order of the map.

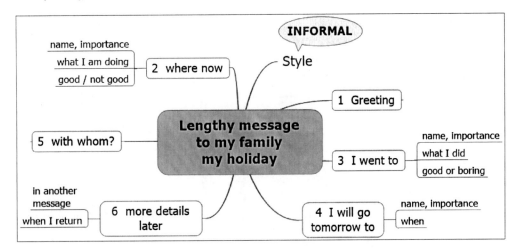

Obviously, <u>it is better to be more specific</u> and to write the specific names of places and people, and your views. In this way, when you are actually writing, you will only be concerned with vocabulary and structure.

It is ESSENTIAL that you do not lose sight of the STYLE required. If you are attending to Question 1 in the GCSE writing examinations (2017 specification), you need to write in an INFORMAL style. The above example is surely a text that you will write in an informal style, but reminding yourself of that is a good precaution – this is the function of the added sub-branch 'style' with the 'INFORMAL' callout bit.

سؤال 2 – أكتب، 130–150 كلمة، كيف، وأنت في طريقك إلى السينما، تعرضت إلى السرقة/ النشل، والذي حدث بعد ذلك، موضحًا أفعالك وشعورك.

Question 2 - Write, in 130-150 words, how, while on your way to the cinema, you were mugged and what happened after that, explaining what you did and your feelings.

As we did with Question 1, the following mind-map can be written in English, but thinking in Arabic from the outset is better.

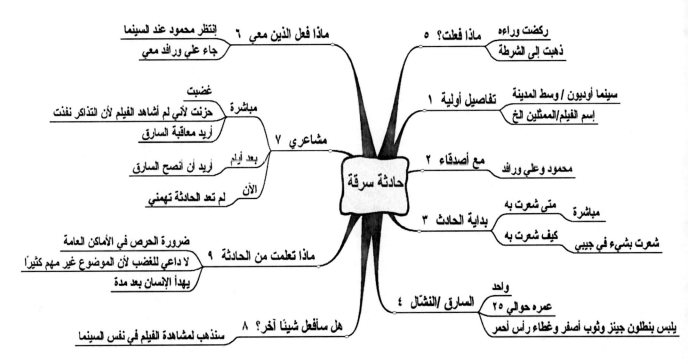

In the examination, you should write the specific details that you are going to include, not all of the possibilities of the above mind-map; hence the following specific mind-map, which should only take few minutes.

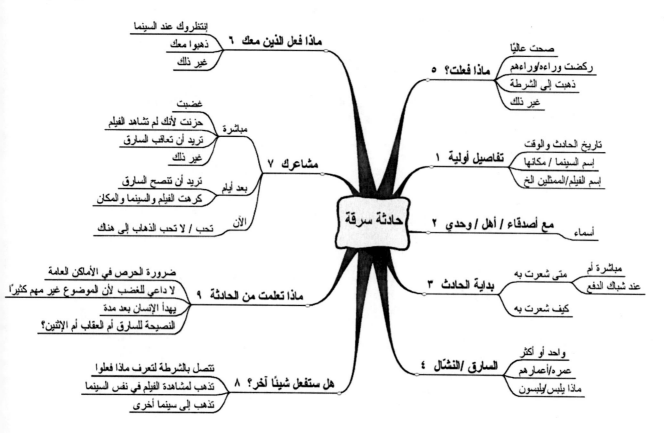

In addition to the details in your quick mind-map, <u>you can enter the **number of words**</u> for each <u>branch</u>. In this way, you know how much you need to write for each point, achieving two things: balancing the size of each point according to its importance, and writing the expected number of words (which in the new 2017 GCSE specification is more relaxed, as you can write less or more as long as you are fulfilling the requirements of the question; AND using the structures and style that aim for the highest marks.) This is illustrated in this final example.

<u>س 3 – صف، في 130–150 كلمة، مدرستك: موقعها، بناياتها، قاعاتها وصفوفها، مساحاتها الخارجية، نشاطاتها</u>

<u>اللادراسية، وحياتها الطلابية، وشعورك نحوها.</u>

Question 3 – Describe, in 130-150 words, your school: its location, buildings, halls and classrooms and outdoor areas, as well as extra-curricular activities, student life and your feelings towards it.

In this task, you are lucky that the main branches of your mind-map are already given in the question. Hence, you need to quickly draw your mind-map with these branches, then to focus on the sub-branches. In the suggested mind-map, the number of words thought suitable for each branch is included.

As you can see, the sub-branches contain the usual details, but some will depend on what is available in your school and also on your participation. Needless to say, the last two branches, i.e. student life and your feelings, are very important because they are the only two points which are not purely descriptive. They are included in the question to test your ability to express your feelings, likes and dislikes and, perhaps, your ability to use humour to make your piece more lively. The projected number of words is between 140 and 200, which means that you are above the 130-150 word limit specified.

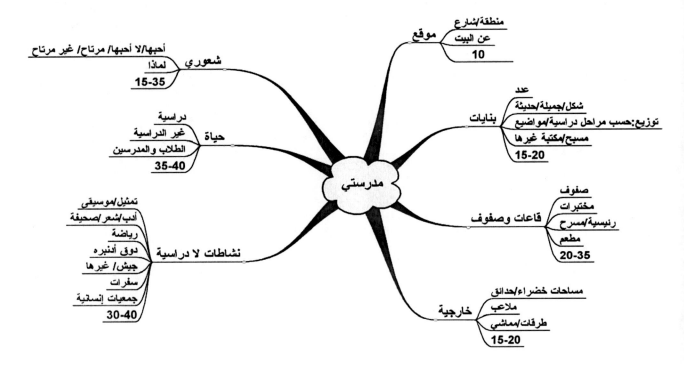

What to do if you are short of words

Your ability to write will vary from one topic to another. Sometimes you will find you have more to say than needed, while at other times you will find yourself struggling to meet the requirements of the question, either in details or in size. In the event that you are short of points or words, you should rely on the relevant ideas, points and details which you can write, or have already written, rather than try to include irrelevant ideas or details just to complete the number of words required. You cannot fool the examiner by including things which are foreign to the question. A piece containing, say, 110 words of relevant, well-written ideas with sound grammatical structure and proper punctuation, though less than the 130-word lower limit of the question, is worth more than one of 200 words which contains anything that comes to your mind, relevant or not. You are better off spending the time available improving your piece, by correcting grammar, punctuation and style. In the following example, we shall see how a piece of writing, which is short of words and ideas, can be improved by expanding on the ideas and details that already exist, and also by using some interesting connecting words.

The school question should not be a problem, so let's try the mugging incident, which some might struggle with. Let's imagine that you wrote the following:

في أحد الأيام كنت ذاهبًا إلى السينما مع أصدقائي. وعندما أردت أن أدفع النقود لشراء التذاكر شعرت بشيء في جيبي، نظرت إلى الوراء رأيت شخصًا يركض. ركضت وراءه ولكني لم أستطع أن ألحق به. ثم ذهبت مع أصدقائي إلى مركز الشرطة وأبلغنا عن الحادثة.

رجعت إلى البيت وأنا حزين. كنت أريد أن أمسك السارق وأعاقبه بنفسي.

في اليوم الثاني اتصل بي صديقي واقترح أن نذهب لمشاهدة الفيلم، ولكني لم أحب أن أذهب إلى نفس المكان مرة أخرى. ولكنه أقنعني بمشاهدة الفيلم في سينما أخرى.

لقد تعلمت من هذه الحادثة ضرورة الحرص في الأماكن العامة المزدحمة.

You check the number of words and find they total around 95 words only. You might think that you need to add more words so that your piece is not much shorter than what is expected, so you look carefully at every sentence and paragraph and introduce the following words (printed in bold).

في أحد الأيام كنت ذاهبًا إلى السينما مع أصدقائي محمود وعلي ورافد، لمشاهدة فيلم من أفلام المافيا. وعندما أردت أن أدفع النقود لشراء التذاكر شعرت بشيء في جيبي، فنظرت إلى الوراء وإذا برجل يركض يلبس سروال جينـز وقميصًا أصفر وغطاء رأس أحمر. مددت يدي إلى جيبي فاكتشفت أن محفظتي غير موجودة. مباشرة ركضت وراءه في عدة شوارع ولكني لم أستطع أن ألحق به لأنه كان أسرع مني.

لذا، ذهبنا إلى مركز الشرطة وأبلغنا عن الحادثة، إلا أن الشرطي قال إن استرجاع المحفظة سيكون صعبًا.

رجعت إلى البيت حزينًا لأني كنت أريد مشاهدة الفيلم الذي سمعت عنه كثيرًا. كنت أريد أن أمسك السارق بيدي وأدخله السجن بنفسي.

في اليوم الثاني اتصل بي رافد واقترح أن نذهب لمشاهدة الفيلم، ولكني لم أحب الذهاب إلى نفس المكان مرة أخرى. ولكنه أقنعني بمشاهدة الفيلم في سينما أخرى. وبالفعل، ذهبنا وكان الفيلم جميلاً، حتى قال محمود أنه يستحق كل هذه المشاكل!

لقد تعلمت من هذه الحادثة ضرورة الحرص في الأماكن العامة، ولا سيما المزدحمة. وأهم من ذلك أن الغضب يهدأ بعد أيام وتعود الحياة إلى مجراها.

You can see that no additional point has been added, but the existing ones have been expanded with details or in style, bringing the total up to 171 words – more than you need. Note how we can replace some words with better alternatives:

ثم ذهبت لذا، ذهبنا	رافد	صديقي	حزينًا وأنا حزين	الذهاب أن أذهب

Note also that including the number of words in your planning mind-map helps to direct your attention to the paragraphs where the idea or point should be expanded, in detail or otherwise, so that you can fill each paragraph with the appropriate number of words.

القسم الثاني

الكتابة في المواضيع المختلفة

5 الكتابة بأسلوب غير رسمي

6 الكتابة بأسلوب رسمي

PART TWO

Topic-related Writing

5 Informal writing

6 Formal writing

الكتابة في المواضيع المختلفة ـ مقدمة

Topic-based Writing

The two chapters of PART 2 deal with writing on different topics (which makes it suitable for Questions 1 and 2 of the 2017 GCSE specification Writing Paper). Since sitting examinations calls for more care from a guide such as this than examination-free learning, the following requirements and exercises take this specification into consideration so that candidates of these examinations can safely benefit from the teaching provided in the two Chapters of Part 4; other users of the book will benefit from the fact that they are following a carefully-designed approach to writing as part of Arabic learning at this level.

The common points of Chapters 5 and 6 as presented in this Guide are set out below, with the details specific for each of them given on the first page of each chapter.

Topics: These are based on the Themes and (their sub-themes) of the Edexcel 2017 GCSE Specification. Here they are:

Theme 1: Identity and culture
● **Who am I?**: relationships; when I was younger; what my friends and family are like; what makes a good friend; interests; socialising with friends and family; role models
● **Daily life**: customs and everyday life; food and drink; shopping; social media and technology (use of, advantages and disadvantages)
● **Cultural life**: celebrations and festivals; reading; music; sport; film and television

Theme 2: Local area, holiday and travel
● **Holidays**: preferences; experiences; destinations
● **Travel and tourist transactions**: travel and accommodation; asking for help and dealing with problems; directions; eating out; shopping
● **Town, region and country**: weather; places to see; things to do

Theme 3: School
● **What school is like**: school types; school day; subjects; rules and pressures; celebrating success
● **School activities**: school trips; events and exchanges

Theme 4: Future aspirations, study and work
● **Using languages beyond the classroom**: forming relationships; travel; employment
● **Ambitions**: further study; volunteering; training
● **Work**: jobs, careers and professions

Theme 5: International and global dimension
● **Bringing the world together**: sports events; music events; campaigns and good causes
● **Environmental issues**: being 'green'; access to natural resources

Notes on the writing pieces provision

(1) The number of words in the suggested answers totals much more than the 80-90 words specified in the guideline. This is for two reasons. The <u>first</u> is so that the answer includes a variety of verbs, nouns, and descriptive and connecting words so that students may use these according to their abilities. The <u>second</u> is to enable some students to memorize parts of the suggested answers, according to the capacity of their memory.

(2) Students may find that the best way to exercise writing is to rewrite the suggested answers, but with changes introduced - for example, by changing some of the words, summarizing some paragraphs and expanding others, or changing the idea, but within the requirements of the question. Also, students should be encouraged to search for other pieces written in the Themes according to Edexcel GCSE specification - such as those found in the textbook "Sadeequkal Arabi" (Your Arabic Friend 2017) or in any other suitable source - and to extract the topics which are appropriate for writing articles, letters or reports at this length and to try to write on these topics, benefiting also from the suggested pieces in this chapter, especially those which are on similar topics.

(3) These two writing chapters feature:

(a) Mind-maps instead of written pieces, or in addition to them, especially in the tasks where students might have difficulty writing about the subject in question. Mind-maps are in either Arabic or English and students are asked to use these mind-maps to complete the writing task.

(b) Providing opening sentences or starters to help with ideas or hints to ideas. For some tasks this approach is added to suggested mind-maps.

(c) At the end of each piece, there are one or more exercises, of the following types:

(c.1) Studying the piece to check how it was successful in satisfying the requirements of the task by determining which paragraphs or sentences relate to which part of the task. This exercise encourages studying the piece, not merely reading it.

(c.2) How can the written pieces be improved? This encourages students to look even more closely - here they have to look into parts of paragraphs, even sentences, to try to replace, omit or add words or phrases to make the piece better.

(c.3) Writing another similar piece, either based on the student's own personal experience (which are pieces that include description of a show or occasion or the like), or based on the student's opinions and suggestions.

(c.4) Trying to condense the given piece while preserving the main points. This encourages students to study the piece closely to see which points are the most important and so should be preserved, and which are less important and so can be omitted. This process calls for changes in vocabulary and structure to the benefit of the teaching goal.

(c.5) The grammar of words or sentences, which aims to remind users of this guide not to overlook grammar while teaching or studying the suggested pieces. This is just a very small contribution to grammar that should be attended to in a more serious way by using our book The Grammar and Translation Guide 2017 or other similar publications.

(c.6) Translation of words, which is a sort of example of how teachers should use the written pieces to test their students' understanding of specific words, whether the one that are part of the task or the ones used as connectives.

(c.7) Using photo stimulus, either to give more depth to the suggested piece, mind-map or opening statements, or as an exercise to write another piece within the same topic.

This variety of exercises should help in choosing the ones that relate to the areas where the student or the user of the book seems to be struggling or in need of more support.

Chapter Five   الفصل الخامس

الكتابة بأسلوب غير رسمي

Informal Writing

Length: 80-90 words

This is only 'recommended', i.e. a guideline, and 'Students will not be penalised for writing more or fewer words than recommended in the word count or for going beyond the mandatory bullets.'

Options: Two options; students must answer one only.

Type of writing: Informal register (or style).

Topics: The Specification Themes (and their sub-themes) of the Edexcel 2017 GCSE Specification.

Assessment: The question 'assesses students on their ability to convey information, narrate, express opinions, interest, and convince the reader about a certain point.'

IMPORTANT: Please refer to the Edexcel 2017 Specification for a detailed description of how marks are awarded for this question.

IDENTITY AND CULTURE

غ.رسمية–1 أكتب، 80–90 كلمة، عن الصداقة:

(أ) من الذين تفضل الخروج معهم؟

(ب) ماذا فعلت مع أصدقائك مؤخراً؟

(ت) ما الذي تخططون لفعله في عطلة نهاية الأسبوع؟

(ث) ما هي الصفات التي تفضلها في صديقك؟

INF-1 Write, in 80-90 words, about friendship: (a) With whom you like to go out? (b) What did you do with your friends lately? (c) What plans for the weekend you and your friends have? And (d) what things do you prefer to find in your friend?

Let's start here by drawing a mind-map containing the ideas, giving some details.

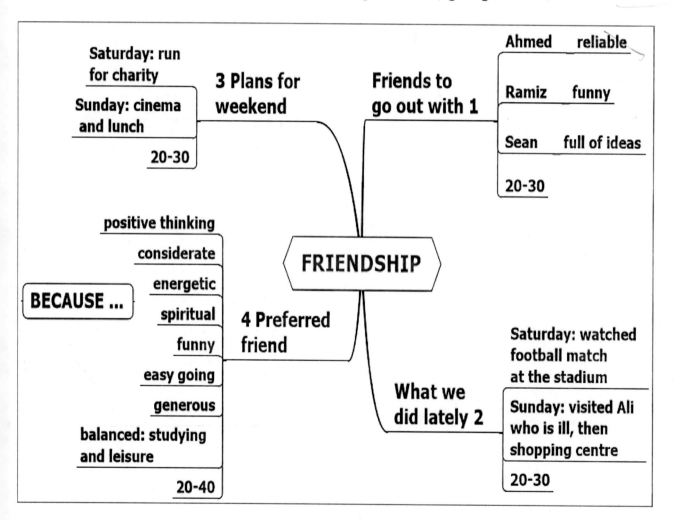

You can see that this mind-map allocates one branch for each part of the task. You can attend to these four parts of the task in any manner, such as mentioning all of the 'preferred friend' list with branch 1 that is listing the friends you like to go out with - to say why you like to go out with them.

Use this mind-map to write the article. The following suggested opening statements uses this mind-map to write the article:

عندي أصدقاء كثيرون، ولكني أحب الخروج مع ...

فإن أحمد يعتمد عليه، خصوصاً ... أما رامز فهو ... شون جدّي أكثر، ولكن أفكاره – نعمل كذا، نذهب إلى كذا – لا تنتهي.

شون شجعنا يوم السبت الفائت على الذهاب إلى الملعب لمشاهدة ...

بعد الدراسة يوم الأحد، ذهبنا لزيارة علي – المسكين كان مريضاً ...

أظن نهاية الأسبوع القادم سيكون منوعاً أيضاً. فبعد التعب من ركض نصف ماراثون لدعم جمعية خيرية، سنذهب الأحد إلى السينما ...

أنا محظوظ بأصدقائي، فيهم الصفات التي أحبها – التفكير الإيجابي، و ...

وذلك لأن ...

You should try to avoid writing the details above as shown, in bullet points or similar. Instead, write them in paragraphs of balanced sizes, with good structure benefiting from varied grammatical forms and the use of connecting words.

<u>Exercise 1</u> Try to condense your piece - expected to be around 120-150 words (if completing the above opening statements) - to reduce it to around 90 words, while preserving the main points.

<u>Exercise 2</u> Write a similar article, around 80-90 words, using other characteristics of good or not-so-good friends, perhaps by using the following table:

يمتلك روح الدُّعابة و المرح (مرح) Funny/has the sense of humour	مَوْثوق/يُعتمَد عليه reliable	أمين honest
مُتفائِل optimistic	مُتَفَهِّم understanding	مُتَواضِع down-to-earth
مُتَشائِم pessimistic	فاتِن /جَذّاب charming	حَسّاس sensitive
ثَرْثار chatty	مُبهج/مُبتَهِج/مَرِح cheerful	مُخْلِص faithful/loyal

❖ After writing your articles, have them corrected by your teacher. Then rewrite them with the corrections and improvements, and keep them in your writing file.

غ.رسمية-2 في حوالي 80-90 كلمة أكتب مقالة بعنوان "عندما كنت صغيراً"، تذكر فيها:

(أ) أوصافك البدنية (ب) أوصافك العقلية (ت) أوصافك الخُلقية

و (ث) ما يقوله أهلك عن أيام طفولتك.

INF-2 Write, in around 80-90 words, an article entitled 'When I was young', mentioning your features and characteristics (a) physical, (b) mental, (c) as revealed in your behaviour, and (d) what your family say about how you were during your childhood.

If you like, you can use some of the following paragraphs and sentences as starters or to give you ideas for writing this article.

عندما كنت صغيرة، أقصد في الابتدائية، كان شعري ...

أبرز (most distinguished) صفة عندي كانت ...

يتفق الأهل على أني كنت كثيرة الحركة، ...

عصام، أخي الكبير، يذكر دائماً ما حصل في يوم ...

في الحقيقة لا أتذكر هذا جيداً، لذلك أقول ...

Try to use interesting 'connective words' such as في الحقيقة, أقصد and لذلك used above to

link the sentences in a way that flows well. Being informal doesn't mean not paying attention also to your punctuation. Legible handwriting is obviously a must.

Exercise 1 Translate the underlined words.

Exercise 2 What grammatical position does each of the words in bold have?

أبرز ، الأهل ، عصام

Exercise 3 Write about your brother or sister, or a close cousin or neighbour whom you knew well when they were young? Try, in 80-90 words:
 (a) writing a similar article to the one you have completed above, about one of them,
 (b) supporting it from personal experience or otherwise,
 (c) then show it to them to see how much they agree with what you have said.

❖ After writing your articles, have them corrected by your teacher. Then rewrite them with the corrections and improvements, and keep them in your writing file.

غ.رسمية-3 أكتب، في حوالي 80-90 كلمة، عن عاداتك في التسوق:

(أ) ماذا (ب) من أين (ت) متى

و (ث) الكلفة من مصروفك الشهري وهل أنك بحاجة إلى إعادة نظر فيها.

INF-3 Write, in around 80-90 words, about your shopping habits: (a) what, (b) from where, (c) when, (d) the cost to your monthly allowance and whether you need to rethink these habits.

If you like, you can use some of the following paragraphs and sentences as starters or to give you ideas for writing this article.

لا يمر أسبوع إلا وأجد نفسي في السوق! أحياناً ...

أعترف أنني أنفق أكثر من اللازم، ولكن ...

لهذا، أفكر في وضع مبلغ ...

المشكلة ليست فقط في حبي للملابس، خصوصاً ...

ولكن صار التسوق – والتنزيلات – معي على شاشة الكومبيوتر! المحلات ...

As you can see, you don't need to attend to the points of the task according to their sequence in the question; the starters above attended to the points in the following order: c – d – d (second bit) - a - b. What is important is not to omit any of them.

Try to use interesting 'connective words' such as خصوصاً and ولكن, أحياناً, used above to link the sentences in a way that flows well. See how good it is to reply to point d of the task by starting with أعترف. Note also the use of the word والتنزيلات, which tells us that shopping has not only become easier with the internet, but that sales are always advertised, making shopping even easier and possibly more addictive.

Don't overlook your punctuation and handwriting.

<u>Exercise</u> 'I <u>have</u> to buy <u>before the sale ends</u>' is something that we must have heard so many times. The photo above sheds some light on the why people say that and how they are driven (or you may say 'tricked') into this. What are your views on this experience, which has turned the sale season into an all-year-round season!
(Around 80-90 words)

❖ After writing your articles, have them corrected by your teacher. Then rewrite them with the corrections and improvements, and keep them in your writing file.

غ.رسمية-4 "على الرغم من الزيادة في عدد القراء الشباب للصحف والمجلات بعد أن صارت على شبكة الانترنت فإن اتجاهاً ينمو لحالة من الاستخدام مرة واحدة بقراءة سطحية متعجّلة لعدد كبير من المقتطفات القصيرة دون فائدة حقيقية. " هل توافق أو لا توافق على أي من القسمين؟ ناقش هذا في حوالي 80-90 كلمة.

INF-4 'Although newspaper and magazine readership among young people has increased since they became online, a sort of disposable information culture is growing where lots of short snippets are scanned hurriedly to no real benefit.' Do you agree or disagree to either of the two parts of this statement? Discuss this in around 80-90 words.

من تجربتي الشخصية وأصدقائي، الشباب يقرأون الصحف أكثر من السابق لأنهم يجدونها في مواقِعها (their websites)، أحياناً بدون قصد (unintentionally) مثلاً أثناء البحث عن معلومة لواجب مدرسي أو بضائع. أما المجلات فلا أوافق، لأن الشباب يحبون مطالعة (reading) مواضيع المجلات، إضافة إلى صورها الملوّنة.

وأكيد أن كثرة الأخبار والتقارير تشجع على قراءة سريعة فتتَبَخَّر المعلومات بسرعة. وهذا أشد عند القراءة من عشرات الصحف على الانترنت، نقفز بين الصحف في ثوانٍ والنتيجة فائدة قليلة. طيب كيف نعالج هذا؟ شخصياً، أقوم بنَسخ ولَصق (copy and paste) ما أريد ليبقى عندي، أقرأه دون عجلة (وبحروف أكبر حتى لا ألبس نظارات مبكّراً!).

لذلك، على المسؤولين في الصّحافة ووكالات الأنباء (news agencies)، من الصّحفيين (journalists) والمُحَرّرين (editors)، تقديم الأخبار والتقارير (reports) بشكل مُوجَز (brief) حتى لا نقفز بسرعة من هذا الخبر إلى تلك المقالة إلى ذلك الإعلان بحيث نُطالِع (read) ما نَشَرَت (published) الجريدة ثم ننسى مباشرة!   (127 كلمة)

Exercise 1 Study the piece above and check how successful it was in satisfying the requirements of the task. Use colour highlighting or another form of marking for quick future reference (different underlining styles are used to highlight connective words, fillers and useful words).

Exercise 2 What grammatical position does each of the words in bold have?

الشباب ، سريعة ، هذا ، حتى لا يقفز

Exercise 3 Write a similar article, perhaps by first drawing a mind-map. You may use the same points and details as shown in the suggested piece above. Or better still, try to write your own discussion, ideas, opinions and suggestions.

❖ After writing your articles, have them corrected by your teacher. Then rewrite them with the corrections and improvements, and keep them in your writing file.

غ.رسمية-5 "مراسيم الزواج هي نفسها سواء أكانت عربية أو بريطانية". تناولي، في نحو 80-90 كلمة،

هذه المقولة ضمن رسالة إلى والديك وأسرتك:

(أ) تصفين فيها عرس ابنة عمتك الذي حضرتيه في بلد عربي

(ب) بالمقارنة مع عرس بريطاني حضرتيه أو شاهدتيه

(ت) وهل أن المقارنة تساهم في تفهّم الناس بعضهم البعض.

INF-5 'A marriage ceremony is a marriage ceremony: there is no difference between Arab and British marriage ceremonies.' Respond to this statement within a letter to your parents and family (a) describing your cousin's wedding which you attended in an Arab country, and (b) comparing it to any British wedding you have attended or saw; and (c) say whether such comparison contributes to greater understanding between people.
(Around 80-90 words)

بعد أن جاء القاضي (the judge) وحكى مع زينب في غرفة مجاورة خرج وأجرى عقد الزواج (the marriage contract). ذكّرتني هذه الطّقوس (rituals) بعُرس آمال عندنا عدا أن العروسين كانا يقفان أمام القسّ والحاضرين، ولكن الجوّ الديني كان متشابهاً.

بعدها ذهبنا إلى الفندق. كانت القاعة مرتّبة والطاولات مفروشة بالورد. دخلت زينب لابسة بدلة عرس بيضاء ذات ذيل طويل وظهرت جميلة جداً.

أما الطعام فقد كان عربياً – أطباق لبنانية وغيرها. إلاّ أن الأجمل كان كعكة العرس المكونة من خمسة طوابق مزينة.

يعني مثل برامج تخطيط (planning) الأعراس على التلفزيون البريطاني – الفرق في عرس زينب الاهتمام بالطعام وكثرته مبالغ فيه، بينما العرس الانجليزي ربما يهتم أكثر بالغناء والرقص.

إستمرت الحفلة حتى ساعة متأخّرة من الليل وقضى الجميع وقتاً طيباً. إشتركت الحاضرات في جوّ الموسيقى والأغاني الشعبية المعروفة للأعراس وبعض الأهازيج الدينية.

صوّر المصوّر شريطاً كاملاً للعرس. رؤوف ابن عمتي أخذ صوراً كثيرة للعروس (bride) والعريس

(groom).

عندما خرجنا قالت مَروة: "أرى أقرباءنا يفرحون في أعراسهم مثل الانجليز!". أَيّدتها، وأننا لا نحكم

(judge) على الآخرين، لأن – <u>ببساطة</u> – الناس يتشابهون في فرحهم وحزنهم فلماذا ننظر إليهم وكأنهم من

كَوكب آخر؟ (166 كلمة)

Exercise 1 Study the piece above and check how successful it was in satisfying the requirements of the task by determining which paragraphs or sentences relate to which part of the task. Use colour highlighting or another form of marking for quick future reference (different underlining styles are used to highlight connective words, fillers and useful words).

Exercise 2 What grammatical position does each of the words in bold have?

متشابهاً ، كعكة ، الجميع ، كوكب

Exercise 3 Translate the following underlined words:

عدا أن ، بعدها ، إلا أن ، يعني ، الفرق ، ربما ، حتى ساعة متأخرة ، ببساطة

Exercise 4 How can the piece above be improved? Look into ways to make it more balanced:

(i)   in terms of how much is written for each part of the task (you may omit, add or replace words, phrases or full sentences),

(ii)   using other, perhaps better, connective words or fillers,

(iii)   using other words or expressions that you think are better for the description given about that wedding party.

Exercise 5 Try to condense this piece, to reduce it to around 90-120 words, while preserving the main points.

Exercise 6 Write (in around 80-90 words) a similar article, perhaps by first drawing a mind-map, and using, if you wish, similar ideas and detail to those in the suggested piece above, from your own experience, using your own discussion, ideas and opinions.

❖ After writing your articles, have them corrected by your teacher. Then rewrite them with the corrections and improvements, and keep them in your writing file.

غ.رسمية-6 "بدأت حفلات عيد الميلاد تبدو مملّة لي – نفس الاسطوانة: عيد ميلاد سعيد، هدايا، كعك، بالونات، غناء وباقي الأمور!" (أ) وضّحي إذا كنت توافقين أو لا توافقين على هذا الرأي (ب) ولماذا (ت) ربما من خلال وصفك، في حوالي 80-90 كلمة، لواحدة من حفلات عيد ميلادك أو حفلة حضرتها.

INF-6 'Birthdays are becoming quite boring for me - same old story: happy birthday, presents, cakes, balloons, singing and the rest of it!' (a) Say whether you agree or not, and (b) why, (c) perhaps by describing, in around 80-90 words, one of your own birthday parties or one that you have attended.

عندما كنت في الثانية عشرة ذهبت إلى عيد ميلاد سناء. كانت حفلة مسلّية، لعبنا لعبة الكراسي الموسيقية وغيرها. بعض البنات لعبن بالحبل في الحديقة. الهدايا ملفوفة بأوراق وأشرطة ملونة.

كان الطعام شهيّاً (appetizing)، ولكن كعكة الشوكولاته بالفراولة (strawberries) كانت لا تُنسى.

شاهدنا فيلماً مشهوراً إسمه "مَدَغَشقر" (Madagascar)، ولعبنا وتحدثنا، إلى أن جاءت المرطّبات. عند المساء قدّمت لنا سناء هدايا تذكارية، كان نصيبي سِلسِلة مفاتيح (my share) (key ring) فيها قرد مضحك.

حفلة حلوة، أتذكرها مع صور مضحكة ومواقف مُحرجة (embarrassing) حصلت.

إذا سألتني عن اليوم، فإني لا أجد متعة (pleasure) في أعياد الميلاد – بعضها مُمِلّ، والبنات يجلسن كل واحدة أو اثنتين في زاوية وكأنهُنّ غير موجودات معنا.

أيضاً، الهدايا تكلّف كثيراً وبعض البنات لا يرضين بالهدايا إلاّ إذا (unless) كانت غالية كأنّ المهمّ هي الهدية لا التعبير (expression) عن المحبة.

يظهر كنا أكثر بَراءة (more innocent) ونحتفل بلا تَعقيدات (complications)، فلمّا كبُرنا صِرنا لا ننجح في الفرح والتسلية في أعياد الميلاد مثل السابق. (139 كلمة)

<u>Exercise 1</u> Study the piece above and check how successful it was in satisfying the requirements of the task. Different underlining styles are used to highlight connective words, fillers and useful words.

<u>Exercise 2</u> Which of these words in bold are past tense verbs, which are present tense verbs, and which one is not a verb? Explain the grammar of each? لعبن ، يجلسن ، كأنهن ، يرضين

<u>Exercise 3</u> Write a similar article from your own experience, perhaps by first drawing a mind-map. You may use the same points and details as shown in the piece above.

❖ After writing your articles, have them corrected by your teacher. Then rewrite them with the corrections and improvements, and keep them in your writing file.

غ.رسمية-7 في حوالي 80-90 كلمة، أكتب

(أ) عن برامج التلفاز التي تشاهدها بانتظام (ب) مثلاً ما شاهدته ليلة أمس (ت) موضحاً/ مبيناً أسباب ذلك

(ث) وبين رأيك في أنواع البرامج التي تعتقد أنها أكثر مما ينبغي أو أقل مما ينبغي عرضه.

INF-7 Write, in at least 80-90 words, about (a) the TV programmes which you watch regularly, (b) for example what you watched last night, (c) explaining why you do so, and (d) expressing your opinion on whichever types of programme that you think there are either too many of, or too few of.

أحب مشاهدة الدراما التلفزيونية: العاطفية (romantic) والفُكاهية (comedy)، كما أشاهد المسلسلات (soap series) التاريخية العربية – وإن كان عدد حلقات (episodes) **بعضها** أكثر من اللازم.

كما أحب الرياضة كثيراً. وبما أني أفضل مسابقات الساحة والميدان (athletics) فإن أحسن الأوقات هو الصيف، حيث أشاهد البَثّ الحَيّ/ المُباشر (live transmission) للقاءات (meetings) في أوروبا والتي تنقلها الفضائيات (satellite channels)، **وبعضها** من المغرب العربي لأن متسابقي المغرب والجزائر يشتركون فيها.

بعدها كرة قدم الدوري الانجليزي أشاهدها أسبوعياً. كان أمس **موعدها**، ولكني انتقلت في منتصفها إلى مسلسل تعرضه القناة الثانية كان لا بأس به.

صحيح أن بعض الناس لا يحبون الرياضة في التلفاز، ولكن القنوات التلفزيونية كثيرة فيمكنك مشاهدة محطّات (channels) أخرى. على كل حال، الرياضة أفضل من أفلام العُنف (violence) والحروب في الأفلام والأخبار.

أشعر أن هناك حاجة لأعمال درامية راقية أكثر، تطرح المشاكل بشكل هادئ وتساعد المُتَفَرِّج (spectator) على كيفية التعامل مع **مشاكله**. كما توجد حاجة لبرامج فُكاهية تطرح النُّكتة بذكاء لا بتَهريج. (136 كلمة)

Exercise 1 Study the piece above and check how successful it was in satisfying the requirements of the task. Different underlining styles are used to highlight connective words, fillers and useful words.

Exercise 2 To which nouns do the pronouns in the words in bold relate?

بعضها ، وبعضها ، موعدها ، مشاكله

Exercise 3 Write a similar article, perhaps by first drawing a mind-map. You may use the same points and details as shown in the suggested piece above. Or better still, try to write your own discussion, ideas, opinions and suggestions.

❖ After writing your articles, have them corrected by your teacher. Then rewrite them with the corrections and improvements, and keep them in your writing file.

LOCAL AREA, HOLIDAY AND TRAVEL

غ.رسمية-8 البعض يدعي:

"البلدان العربية السياحية غالباً ما تظهر أقل مستوى عندما تزورها عما تسمعه أو تقرؤه عنها".

هل توافق على هذا أم لا توافق؟

أجب، في حوالي 80-90 كلمة، مبرراً وجهة نظرك.

INF-8 'Arab countries that are attractive for tourists are often found to be much inferior when you actually visit them compared to what you hear or read about them', some claim. Do you agree or disagree?
In around 80-90 words justify your answer either way.

في إجازة (holiday) الصيف زرنا مصر. وصلنا القاهرة بالليل والشوارع هادئة، ولكن في الصباح تفاجَأنا (we were surprised) بفُوضى السيارات وعربات تجرّها الحيوانات، وكل يسير مثلما يريد!

زيارة الأهرامات (the Pyramids) أنستنا الشوارع – وجدنا أنفسنا مُنبهرِين (dazzled) بها وبتمثال "أبو الهول" (the Sphinx). بعدها أول مطعم، وتحذير من صديقنا المصري من بعض الأطعمة والأشربة!

ثالث يوم زرنا "خان الخليلي"، السوق الشهير. هناك أيضاً الجانبان: جمال السوق والبضائع وخِفّة دم (wittiness) الباعة (traders)، مع الأسعار المُبالَغ فيها (exaggerated)!

زرنا المتحف المصري المليء بالآثار القديمة أيام الفراعِنة (the Pharaohs)، وقَلعة محمد علي (the Castle of Muhammad Ali) وغيرها، وكلها لا يوجد مثلها في أوروبا.

بعد أيام ذهبنا إلى الإسكندرية على البحر الأبيض المتوسط. على شاطئ "الرُّوّاد" كان البحر صافياً أزرق اللون بشكل لا مَثِيلَ له (unparalleled).

المحطّة الثالثة "شَرْم الشّيخ" جنوب سيناء. ركبنا مركباً أرضيته من زجاج نتفرج من خلاله على الحيوانات والنباتات العجيبة في البحر الأحمر.

بعض المرافق كان أفضل من غيره، وصحيح مستوى الخدمة في بعضها ضعيف، ولكن البعض يجعل "من الحَبّة كُبّة" فينزعج (become annoyed) من كل شيء! طيب لماذا تسافر؟! السفر يعني مكاناً وجوّاً مختلفين، إذاً

تتوقّع (expecting) <u>الإزعاجات</u>. مثلاً، نسمع عن حوادِث (accidents) التّسمّم بالطعام والشراب، والسبب

عدم الاعتياد على البكتيريا هناك، والحلّ سهل: شرب الماء المعدني (mineral water)! (176 كلمة)

Exercise 1 Study the piece above and check how successful it was in satisfying the requirements of the task. Use colour highlighting or another form of marking for quick future reference.

Exercise 2 Write the past tenses in the words in bold in their form before connecting to the pronoun نا: زُرنا ، أنسَتنا ، ذهَبنا ، ركِبنا .

Exercise 3 Translate the following underlined words:

فوضى ، تحذير ، البحر الأبيض المتوسط ، طيب ، الإزعاجات

Exercise 4 How can the piece above be improved? Look into ways to make it more balanced:

(i) in terms of how much is written for each part of the task (you may omit, add or replace words, phrases or full sentences),

(ii) using other, perhaps better, connective words or fillers,

(iii) using other words or expressions that you think are better for the information and description given about this holiday trip.

Exercise 5 Write (in around 80-90 words) a similar article, perhaps by first drawing a mind-map, and using, if you wish, similar ideas and detail to those in the suggested piece above, either:

(a) from your own experience, using your own discussion, ideas and opinions

or

(b) by using a promotional brochure that you picked up from a travel agent to imagine the kind of trip you would like to arrange for your next holiday.

❖ After writing your articles, have them corrected by your teacher. Then rewrite them with the corrections and improvements, and keep them in your writing file.

تبحث عن سفرات إلى الشرق الأوسط والشرق الأقصى؟

الجواب عندنا ! أُطلب تجد !

شقق. شقق فندقية. فنادق. شاليهات.

وحسب المواصفات الدولية المعتمدة.

مواقع في المدينة وعلى البحر وعند مناطق جبلية.

ترتيب رحلات بحرية وفي الجبال والصحراء.

ترتيب زيارة الآثار والمتاحف والمرافق الأخرى.

رحلات داخلية بالقطار والطائرة والمركب.

تخفيض يصل إلى 40٪ على معظم الرحلات.

غ.رسمية-9 أحياناً يعبر السائحون عن خيبة أملهم في الفندق أو المجمع السياحي الذي نزلوا فيه في المرافق والخدمات جميعاً.

(أ) ماذا يمكن لمثل هؤلاء أن يفعلوا في مثل تلك الحالات

(ب) كيف يتجنبونها أساساً

ربما يمكنك (ت) أن تكتب من تجربة شخصية.

أكتب حوالي 80-90 كلمة.

INF-9 Tourists sometimes express their disappointment with their holiday hotel or tourist complex, in both premises and services. (a) What can such tourists do in such situations and (b) how can they avoid them in the first place? (c) You might like to write on this, in around 80-90 words, from personal experience.

أول ما وصلنا إلى الفندق شعرنا أننا ارتَكَبنا (we committed) خطئاً كبيراً. كان المَدخَل (entrance) حديثاً، ولكن الغرفة مظلمة والأثاث قبيح يختلف عن الصور عند وكيل السفريات (travel agent).

في كل غرفة جهاز تلفزيون فيه المحطات المحلّية (local) وليس فيه حتى ولا محطات فضائية (satellite) مجانية. بقي أخي سامح يقلّب القنوات (channels) دُون جَدوى/ عَبَثاً (in vain)!

كان المطعم خادعاً، فالأثاث جميل لكن الطعام من أسوأ ما أكلت. "لا نريد هذا الطبق... أبدله بآخر ساخن... هذا لم نطلبه..." النتيجة: صرنا نتناول الإفطار فقط رغم أن السفرة تتضمن وجبة أخرى.

كان بعض موظفي الفندق يُسرعون لتلبية طلباتنا (rush to attend to our requests)، غيرهم وجوههم منقبضة دائماً! وقد أضعنا وقتاً كثيراً باتّباع إرشاداتهم (their instructions) الخطأ لزيارة المناطق السياحية.

حاولنا تغيير الغرفة، طلبوا انتظار أن تفرغ غرفة وطلبوا مبلغاً إضافياً. ننتظر إلى متى؟ إنتقلنا إلى فندق آخر كي لا نضيع الوقت.

في النهاية، إعترف أبي أنه حجز السفرة بناءً على (based on) إعلان يعرض سعراً مُغرياً (tempting/attractive) فلم يسأل عن الفندق. بعبارة أخرى، أراد دفع كلفة أقل فانتهى إلى سفرة تساوي حتى أقل مما دفع. لعل أبي يحتاج إلى ما كانت تقوله جدّتي: "الغالي رَخيص!"، وما جاء في الحديث ((ما خابَ مَنِ استَشار)).   (170 كلمة)

Exercise 1 Study the piece above and check how successful it was in satisfying the requirements of the task by determining which paragraphs or sentences relate to which part of the task. Use colour highlighting or another form of marking for quick future reference (different underlining styles are used to highlight connective words, fillers and useful words).

Exercise 2 What is the meaning of the sentences in bold?

((ما خاب من استشار)) ، الغالي رخيص

Exercise 3 What grammatical position does each of the words in bold have?

جميل ، منقبضة ، غرفة ، أبي

Exercise 4 How can the piece above be improved? Look into ways to make it more balanced:

(i)   in terms of how much is written for each part of the task (you may omit, add or replace words, phrases or full sentences),

(ii)   using other, perhaps better, connective words or fillers,

(iii) using other words or expressions that you think are better for the description given about that experience.

Exercise 5 Write (in around 80-90 words) a similar article, perhaps by first drawing a mind-map, and using, if you wish, similar ideas and detail to those in the suggested piece above, either:

(a) from your own experience, using your own discussion, ideas, opinions and suggestions

or

(b) by describing the feelings of the people who wrote this negative review of their holiday, adding any detail that comes to your mind when imagining the kind of bad experience they have suffered.

إيّاكم ثم إيّاكم أن تذهبوا إلى هذا الفندق!

كل شيء تقريباً سيء!

الغرف قبيحة وصغيرة، والمنظر على موقف سيارات — لم نحجز غرفة في كراج!

المطعم قديم، والطعام سنة إلى أن يأتي، ويوم لا بأس به ويوم رديء.

نعم، الموظفون يبتسمون — ولكن لا أدري لماذا وحال الفندق هكذا!

باختصار: فندق مزبلة، ولو كان هناك تقييم أقل من "صفر" لأثّرت عليه!!!

❖ After writing your articles, have them corrected by your teacher. Then rewrite them with the corrections and improvements, and keep them in your writing file.

غ.رسمية-10 الخريطة تبين شوارع وأبنية، وامرأة خرجت من "محطة قطار"، واقفة عند "إشارة مرور" مقابل عمارة سكنية 1"، تسأل سليم عن كيفية الوصول إلى (أ) "عمارة سكنية 3"، ثم إلى (ب) "النادي" من مدخله المؤشر بسهم. أكمل، في ما مجموعه حوالي 80-90 كلمة، ما شرحه سليم لكيفية الوصول إلى الموقعين.

INF-10 The map shows streets and buildings and a woman who, after coming out of the 'train station', stands at the 'traffic lights' facing the 'residential building 1', and asks Seleem directions to go to (a) 'residential building 3', and after that to (b) the 'club', the entrance of which is denoted by an arrow. In <u>a total of 80-90 words</u> complete Seleem's directions to <u>both places</u>.

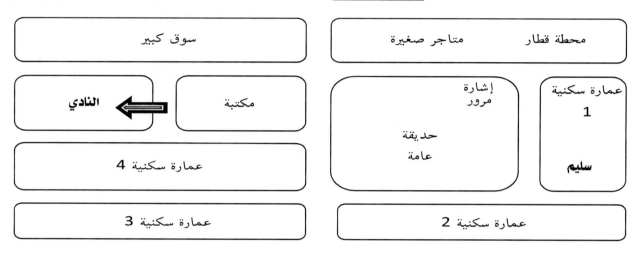

سيري <u>باتجاه</u> عمارة ...   ثم انعطفي (turn) إلى ...

وسيري حتى <u>تصلي</u> إلى ... إستمرّي بالسير (keep walking) وتَخَطّي (pass) ...

إلى أن <u>تجدي</u> باب العمارة على <u>جهة</u> ...

إذا أردت الذهاب من هناك إلى النادي، <u>أخرجي</u> ...

وعند التقاطُع (junction) ...

<u>واشي</u> حتى .... هناك <u>أدخلي</u> ...

ثم عند تقاطع ...

وسيكون مدخل النادي <u>أمامك</u>.

<u>Exercise</u> Use the same map to give directions to your friend who is coming, by train, to visit you, at your flat in 'Res. Bldg. 4' - the entrance is opposite to 'Res. Bldg. 3'.

❖ After writing the directions, have them corrected by your teacher. Then rewrite them with the corrections and improvements, and keep them in your writing file.

غ.رسمية-11 الأمهات يقلقن على ما يأكله أولادهن عندما يكونون وحدهم في رحلة أو مخيم، على أساس أنهم سوف لا يأكلون غير الأطعمة الجاهزة غير الصحية. ماذا يمكن لهن أو للمدرسة أن يفعلوا لتشجيعهم على تناول طعام صحي أو حتى طبخ بعض الوجبات الخفيفة في مثل هذه الحالات؟

أكتبي حوالي 80-90 كلمة.

INF-11 Mothers worry about their children's diet when they are on their own on a trip or at a camp, thinking that they will only eat ready-made junk food. What can they or the school do to encourage them to eat healthy food, or even to cook some light meals in such situations? Write around 80-90 words.

الأكل في السفرات مسألة عويصة (quite hard)! فكرة تعلّم طبخة من اللحم أو السمك لا يتقبّلها الكثير من المراهقين – قِدر طهي (cooking pot) وأدوات المطبخ وكمّيّات محدّدة وبتسلسُل (sequence) معيّن، وكل ذلك يستغرق وقتاً (takes time) والنتيجة غير مَضمونة (not guaranteed)! تصوّري هذا في سفرة يريدون أن يستغلّوا (use) كل دقيقة منها للعب والتسلية – طبعاً شيء مستحيل!

"أقصى شيء ساندويتشة من الخبز والجبنة!" سيقول أحدهم... "لا لا، أستطيع عمل بَيض مَقليّ (fried eggs)!" سيقول آخر له معرِفة بالطبخ!

بالحقيقة، لا داعيَ (no need) لوضع قائمة طعام (menu) طويلة عريضة لأن القليل من الأولاد والبنات في هذه الأعمار يحبون أن يقضوا (spend) وقتاً طويلاً في الطبخ، أو حتى تعلم بعض الطبخات. ولكن يمكنهم أن يكتشفوا أن تحضير وجبات خفيفة من الخضروات أو السَّلَطة والسّمك المشوي (grilled) بالفرن ممكناً.

طيب، والنشاطات خارج المخيّم أو السكن؟ سهلة: ساندويتشات الجبنة أو البيض والبطاطا مع بعض الفواكه والحليب أو العصير. المهم لا نضعهم بين اختيارين: إما الأطعمة الصحّيّة أو الأطعمة السريعة، لأنه يمكن أن تكون الفواكه والخضروات الطازجة (fresh) جزءاً مُحَسِّناً للغذاء الذي يحتاجونه للطاقة والقوة في نشاطات السفرات والرحلات. (157 كلمة)

Exercise 1 Study the piece above and check how successful it was in satisfying the requirements of the task by determining which paragraphs or sentences relate to which part of the task. Use colour highlighting or another form of marking for quick future reference (different underlining styles are used to highlight connective words, fillers and useful words).

Exercise 2

(a) What is the grammar of the verbs in the phrases in bold?

(b) How should they be written in a nominal (*ismiyyeh*) form?

أن يكتشفوا ، أن يقضوا ، أن يستغلوا

Exercise 3 Translate the following underlined words: بالحقيقة ، أو حتى ، ممكناً ، محسّناً .

Exercise 4 How can the piece above be improved? Look into ways to make it more balanced:

(i)   in terms of how much is written for each part of the task (you may omit, add or replace words, phrases or full sentences),

(ii)   using other, perhaps better, connective words or fillers,

(iii)   using other words or expressions that you think are better for the description and ideas given about this common issue.

Exercise 5 Try to condense this piece, to reduce it to around 100-120 words, while preserving the main points (remember that the 80-90 words in the examination is only a guideline - you may write more.).

Exercise 6 Write (in around 80-90 words) a similar article, perhaps by first drawing a mind-map, and using, if you wish, similar ideas and detail to those in the suggested piece above, either:

(a) from your own experience, using your own discussion, ideas, opinions and suggestions

or

(b) by responding to this situation: your relative or neighbour and her son, whom you are visiting, are engaged in a lively dispute over food and eating, just one day before he is due to go on a four-day boat trip with his mates, and they invite you to express your opinion, with a little bit of pressure from each of them to side with them!

❖ After writing your articles, have them corrected by your teacher. Then rewrite them with the corrections and improvements, and keep them in your writing file.

غ.رسمية-12 عندما تسافرين – أنت أو أهلك – إلى الخارج كيف تتسوقون؟ أكتبي،80-90 كلمة، عن هذا الموضوع، بتناول النقاط التالية:

(أ) ما يحتاج إليه المسافر (ب) أماكن التسوق والأسعار

(ت) الأشياء التي تشترينها أو يمكن أن تشتريها

(ث) هل أن التسوق مهم مثل زيارة المعالم المهمة أم لا، ولماذا؟

INF-12 Write, in 80-90 words, about shopping when travelling: (a) what travellers need, (b) places and prices, (c) what you have bought or would buy, and (d) whether or not shopping is as important as visiting tourist attractions, and why?

Let's start here by drawing a mind-map containing the ideas, giving some details.

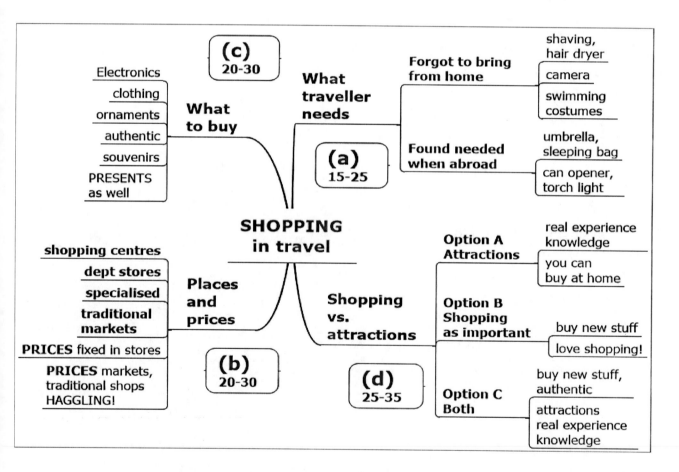

You can see that this mind-map allocates one branch for each part of the task. However, it was brainstormed without regard to sequence, then the task parts a, b, c and d were added, along with estimated number of words. For branch d, you are expected to choose one option only, but you can mention what other people, who would choose the other options, think.

This mind-map contains alternatives. Your mind-map should be smaller and more customized. It could look like this:

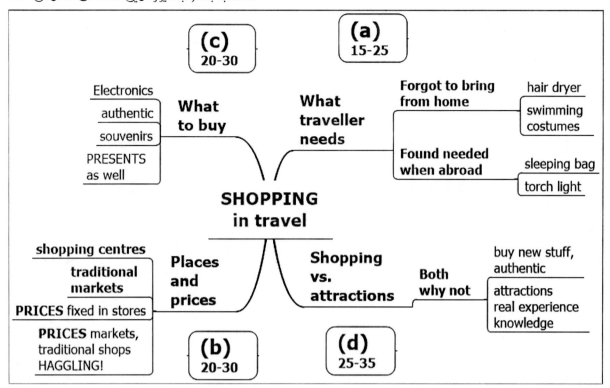

It should be noted that the time spent in drawing such a full and detailed mind-map is well spent, since what is left is just a matter of putting the information entered in the branches into sentences, with good fillers/connective words and adding interesting opening words or thought-provoking comments. In other words, your piece is already half-written (this is in addition to the main point of mind-mapping, which is not forgetting to include all relevant points.)

Use this mind-map to write the article, but you should try to avoid writing the above details as they are, in bullet points or similar. Instead, write them in paragraphs of balanced sizes, with good structure benefiting from varied grammatical forms and the use of connecting words.

Exercise What would you do if you found yourself, like the girl who has sent this WhatsApp message to her sister, travelling with two friends, who, in addition to their conflicting tastes, are not as keen as you are to spend precious time on visiting the tourist attractions of the area, including monuments and other heritage sites? (80-90 words)

إرتكبت أكبر غلطة بحياتي... ما يكفي أن ذوقي في وادي وهما في وادي آخر بحيث لا أقترح شيئاً إلا ويرفض فأضطر إلى اقتراح غيره مما ربها يعجبهما، ما يكفي هذا ليدمر السفرة وإذا أجد أن كل واحدة تريد شيء الثانية تعارضها، كأنه بشكل مقصود، بحيث لا نتفق على زيارة مكان أو مطعم أو غيره إلا بعد نقاش طويل يصل إلى العراك! لا أدري والله لماذا قالتا أنهما يحبان ما أحب وتريدان زيارة معالم البلد، تبين أن المعالم عندهما: المقهى والسوق!

❖ After writing your articles, have them corrected by your teacher. Then rewrite them with the corrections and improvements, and keep them in your writing file.

غ.رسمية-13 أكتب، بما مجموعه حوالي 80-90 كلمة، نشرة الطقس المتوقعة:

(أ) لبلد عربي يقع في شمال إفريقيا في الصيف

(ب) مدينة في شمال انجلترا أو اسكتلندا في شهر يناير/ كانون الثاني.

INF-13 Write, in a total of around 80-90 words, the 'expected' weather forecast for: (a) an Arab country in North Africa in summer, (b) a town in northern England or in Scotland in January.

If you like, you can use some of the following phrases as starters or to give you ideas for writing these two weather forecasts. Each piece needs not be more than one or two paragraphs, hence the separation dots between the suggested opening phrases, which should be sequenced in a logical way (the progression duing the day).

Also, the following (incomplete) list of relevant words should prove helpful.

(أ)   بلد عربي شمال إفريقي:

سيكون الطقس .. في المناطق .. بينما يكون .. في المناطق .. أما درجات الحرارة .. أما <u>ما عدا</u> في .. حالة البحر ..

(ب)   مدينة في شمال انجلترا أو اسكتلندا:

تسبب موجة البرد الحالية انخفاضاً .. مع احتمال <u>تساقط</u> .. وفي الصباح يحتمل هطول .. أما مساءً فستكون

السماء .. ولكن ستستمر الحرارة بالانخفاض عن <u>المعدل</u> في مثل ..

رِياح شمالية northerly wind	مُشْمِس sunny	دافئ/ معتدِل warm/mild
درجة الحرارة الصُّغْرى/ العُظمى minimum/maximum temperature	غائِم cloudy	زَخّات مطر showers
الجليد يتَساقَط it is snowing	غائِم جُزئيًا some cloud	بَرق ورَعد lightning and thunder

Try to use interesting 'connective words' such as أما ,بينما, and ولكن used above to link the

sentences in a way that flows well.

<u>Exercise 1</u> Translate the underlined words.

<u>Exercise 2</u> Give the full grammar of the sentence in bold: تسبب موجة البرد الحالية انخفاضاً .

❖ After writing your piece, have it corrected by your teacher. Then rewrite it with the corrections and improvements, and keep it in your writing file.

غ.رسمية-**14** في حوالي 80-90 كلمة،

(أ) أكملي الوصف الذي كتبته غادة والذي بدأته بقولها: (ذهبت مع صديقاتي إلى المسرح في وسط لندن ....)

(ب) ذاكرةً اسم المسرحية وقصتها

(ت) واصفةً المسرح والديكور والموسيقى والتمثيل

(ث) شعورك وشعور المتفرجين

(ج) هل كان يمكن تحسين بعض جوانبها وكيف.

INF-14 In around 80-90 words (a) complete the description that Ghada has started by saying: 'I went with my friends to the theatre in central London...', (b) mention the title of the play and its plotline, (c) describe the theatre, décor, music and acting, and (d) add your feelings and that of the audience; also (e) if there was anything that could be improved and how.

ذهبت مع صديقاتي إلى المسرح <u>وسط</u> لندن، وكان <u>يعرض</u> مسرحية "هامِلِت" للأديب الانجليزي الشهير وليم شيكسبير، وهي حول ما فعله الأمير هامِلِت <u>بعد</u> رؤيته شَبَح (ghost) أبيه وطلبه الانتقام من قتلته (his murderers)؛ <u>أحداث مأساوية</u> (tragic events) تنتهي بمقتل هاملت.

<u>التصميم</u> القديم للمسرح وضعنا في زمان المسرحية، وكانت الكراسي أعلى من المسرح فسهّل علينا الرؤية. أما الموسيقى التي استعملها <u>المُخرِج</u> (director) فساعدت أيضاً، لأنه استعمل الآلات الموسيقية القديمة التي كانت تستخدم قبل أربعة قُرون (centuries). كذلك، كانت <u>الإضاءة</u> (lighting) تتغير <u>أثناء المشاهد</u> وهذا جعل بعضها مُثيرة حقاً (really exciting).

ملابس الممثلين جميلة، بعضها مذهّب ومُطرّز بأحجار ملونة. ولو أن <u>بعضها</u> كان مُبالَغاً فيه (exaggerated).

طبعاً الأهم هي <u>القصة</u> نفسها، <u>والممثلون النُّجُوم</u> (stars) نجحوا في تقديمها (presenting) بشكل جديد فيه جوانب من الوقت الحاضر. أتوقّع (I expect) أن الكثيرين من المتفرجين شاهدوا المسرحية بشكلها الأصلي (in its original format)، وأتوقع أنهم – <u>مثلي</u> – وجدوا بعض التغييرات مبالغاً فيها، <u>بصراحة</u> لم أفهم المقصود (the meaning) منها! هذا أيّده بعض النُّقّاد (critics) <u>حسبما</u> قرأت.

المسرحية كانت ممتعة جداً، ونجحت في <u>دَمجي</u> (make me engage) بالأحداث. نعم، أسعار التذاكر كانت عالية، ولكنها كانت تستحق ذلك. (156 كلمة)

<u>Exercise 1</u> Study the piece above and check how successful it was in satisfying the requirements of the task by determining which paragraphs or sentences relate to which part of the task. Use colour highlighting or another form of marking for quick future reference (different underlining styles are used to highlight connective words, fillers and useful words).

<u>Exercise 2</u> What is the grammar of the words in bold? وسط ، بعد ، قبل ، أثناء

<u>Exercise 3</u> Translate the following underlined words: التصميم ، المشاهد ، القصة ، حسبما.

<u>Exercise 4</u> How can the piece above be improved? Look into ways to make it more balanced:

(i)   in terms of how much is written for each part of the task (you may omit, add or replace words, phrases or full sentences),

(ii)   using other, perhaps better, connective words or fillers,

(iii)   using other words or expressions that you think are better for the description and opinions given about that experience.

<u>Exercise 5</u> Try to condense this piece, to reduce it to around 100 words, while preserving the main points.

<u>Exercise 6</u> Write (in around 80-90 words) a similar article, perhaps by first drawing a mind-map, and using, if you wish, similar ideas and detail to those in the suggested piece above, either:

(a) from your own experience, using your own discussion, ideas, opinions and suggestions

or

(b) by describing the photo of a performance in a theatre of Shakespeare's Julius Caesar. (For the purpose of the exercise, you may refer to any source to give you an idea about the play.)

❖ After writing your articles, have them corrected by your teacher. Then rewrite them with the corrections and improvements, and keep them in your writing file.

غ.رسمية-**15** من خلال وصفك ليوم قضيته في المركز الترفيهي بيّن، في حوالي **80-90** كلمة،

(أ) ما يجذبك أو أصدقاءك أو غيرهم لممارسة هذا النشاط أو ذاك

(ب) لماذا يفضل الكثيرون القيام بتدريباتهم أو قضاء وقت تسليتهم في المركز الترفيهي المحلّي الذي يخدم منطقتهم.

INF-15 Through describing a day you have spent at a leisure centre, explain (a) what attracts you, your friends or others to this or that activity or sport, and (b) why many people prefer to spend their training or leisure time at their local leisure centre. (Around 80-90 words)

ذهبنا، أنا وصديقتي ليلى، إلى المركز الترفيهي في منطقتنا (district/area). دفعنا رَسْمِ الدخول (entrance fee)، وفوراً إلى المسبح – رائع: الماء دافئ، بقينا ساعتين نسبح ونتَزَحلَق (slide) ونقفز في الماء. أكثر مكان أحبه، لأني أشعر وزني خفيف فأستطيع القيام بالحركات المستحيلة على الأرض. أما ليلى فتحب الغَوص (diving)، لذا ترمي قطع النقود ثم تنزل بنظّارات الماء (goggles)، للبحث عنها!

بعد أن جفّفنا (we dried up) أجسامنا ولبسنا ملابسنا، ذهبنا إلى قاعة كرة المضرب/ التنس ولعبنا ساعة. صار الجوع لا يُحتمل! إذاً إلى الكافيتريا. جلسنا قرب أحواض الزهور الجميلة، وتناولنا شيئاً خفيفاً. قابلنا سعاد، وكانت تريد أن تلعب كرة السلة. "أوه إنّي متعبة!" لكنها سحبتنا إلى القاعة وهي تقول: "هل هناك أكثر مَهارة (ability) من إدخال كرة كبيرة في حلقة صغيرة عالية؟!"

هناك وجدنا بعض البنات اللاتي لا نعرفهن، طلبنا أن نلعب معهن فلم يكن لديهنّ مانع (objection).

قبل خروجنا اتصلت أمي وقالت أنها تأخرت وعليّ أن أعود بالباص. لا مشكلة، فمحطة الباص على بعد خُطُوات (steps)، والمسافة إلى البيت قريبة والطريق آمِن (safe). كان يومًا ممتعًا ومفيدًا، ولم يُكلّفنا (costs us) الكثير من المال.

(157 كلمة)

Exercise 1 Study the piece above and check how successful it was in satisfying the requirements of the task by:
(i) determining which paragraphs or sentences relate to which part of the task
(ii) listing the points that relate to each of the two parts of the task.

Exercise 2 Translate the words with wavy underlines.

Exercise 3 Write a similar article from your own experience, perhaps by first drawing a mind-map. You may use the same points and details as shown in the suggested piece above.

❖ After writing your articles, have them corrected by your teacher. Then rewrite them with the corrections and improvements, and keep them in your writing file.

◼◼◼◼◼◼◼◼◼ SCHOOL ◼◼◼◼◼◼◼◼◼

غ.رسمية-16 في حوالي 80-90 كلمة أكتب مقالة حول "قوانين وضغوط المدرسة" بعنوان "آه لو كنت

المدير!" ربما تحبين تناول النقاط التالية:

(أ) إختيار مواضيع الدراسة (ب) الامتحانات (ت) الملابس والزينة (ث) أي نقطة أخرى تجدينها مهمة.

INF-16 In around 80-90 words write an article on 'the school's rules and pressures' entitled 'I wish I was the head teacher!' You might like to attend to the following points: (a) choosing the subjects, (b) examinations, (c) clothes and accessories (and makeup), and (d) any other point you think important.

قوانين في الصف وفي الساحة وحتى خارج المدرسة، ثم يقولون: هذه المدرسة غير مُنضَبِطة (not

disciplined)! مدرستي بحاجة إلى قوانين أقل وليس أكثر.

فهمنا أنه لا يجوز الركض داخل الأبنية، ما معنى "لا تركضنَ في الساحة"؟! أو الالتزام باللباس الرسمي

(uniform)، وملابس مدرستنا حلوة، ولكن ما معنى عدم لبس سِوار (bracelet) أو سلسلة ذهبية؟ نحن

بنات وتعجبنا هذه الأشياء!

الكثير منّا يشعر بضغوط عديدة أصلاً، فعلى المدرسة أن تخفّف الأمور الأخرى. يكفي أن الكثير من البنات

يدرسن مواضيع لا يحبّنها، بينما هناك مواضيع أخرى جميلة مفيدة للعمل فيما بعد لا تُدرَّس عندنا.

طبعاً ضغط الدراسة والامتحانات أشد وأكبر من هذه الدروس التي لا نحبها، وأكيد النتائج لن تكون أحسن

ما يكون، ولكن المدرسين يلوموننا (blame us) نحن على عدم الحصول على درجات عالية.

لو كنت المديرة لقمت باستطلاع (questionnaire) أجمع فيه ما تقوله الطالبات والمدرسات وحتى الأهالي في

هذا الموضوع ثم نتفق (we agree) على أية تغييرات مفيدة.   (139 كلمة)

Exercise 1 Check how successful the piece above was in satisfying the requirements of the task. Use colour highlighting or another form of marking for quick future reference.

Exercise 2 How can this piece be improved? Give two examples.

Exercise 3 For each of the words in bold فهمنا ، تركضن ، تُدرَّس ، يلوموننا

(a) Rewrite it into its constituents (b) Give the grammar of each part.

Exercise 4 In around 80-90 words, write a similar article from your own experience, perhaps by first drawing a mind-map. You may use the same points and details as shown in the suggested piece above.

❖ After writing your articles, have them corrected by your teacher. Then rewrite them with the corrections and improvements, and keep them in your writing file.

غ.رسمية-**17** في حوالي 80-90 كلمة، أكتبي أفكارك وأفكار صديقتين لك للاحتفال بالنجاح والتخرّج بعد نهاية السنة الدراسية. يمكن أن تضمنوها تفاصيل الاحتفال (أ) كيف (ب) أين (ت) مع من و (ث) أية معلومات أخرى.

INF-17 In around 80-90 words, write about your ideas and those of two of your friends on celebrating your success and graduation from school. You may include the details on: (a) how, (b) where, (c) with whom, and (d) any other information.

If you like, you can use some of the following paragraphs and sentences as starters or to give you ideas for writing this article.

أريده احتفالاً لا ينسى، لأننا ...

قالت نادين: موافقة. فما رأيكما لو ذهبنا ...

كعادتها ميرال تعترض: إمم، ممكن، ولكنني أخاف ...

طيب، ما تقولان في ...

هذا جميل ! لقد شاهدت مثله ...

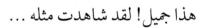

"ها، موافقة؟" أخيراً، اتفقنا على أن نقوم ...

بهذه الطريقة لا ننسى أهلنا الذين ...

As you can see, you don't need to attend to the points of the task according to their sequence in the question; you can mix them as you go along with the piece. But make sure that all points are included.

Since the piece involves including the ideas of two other people, it is up to you to write it as a dialogue with separate lines for the speakers, or, which might be better, to make it a more interesting narrative in which you mention the dialogue selectively. If you follow the second way, you need to make good use of connective words, especially those that can show the excitement of the people who are discussing planning such an important event.

Don't overlook your punctuation and handwriting.

❖ **After writing your article, have it corrected by your teacher. Then rewrite it with the corrections and improvements, and keep it in your writing file.**

غ.رسمية-18 "يمكن لسفرة مدرسية إلى خارج البلاد أن تعلم الطلاب أكثر من فصل دراسي كامل". في حوالي

80-90 كلمة تناول هذه المقولة، بتضمين النقاط التالية:

(أ) كم هي صحيحة أو غير صحيحة

دعم رأيك من خلال (ب) المقارنة مع حصص الدروس أو (ت) وصف موجز لسفرة مدرسية ذهبت فيها.

INF-18 'A school trip abroad can teach students what a full school term cannot.' In around 80-90 words, discuss this statement, including the following points: (a) how correct or incorrect it is, (b) support your opinion through comparison with school lessons or (c) through describing briefly a school trip you have been on.

هذه الجملة صحيحة، <u>ولو مع بعض المُبالغة</u>، لأن الفصل الدراسي يمكن أن يعلم الكثير. <u>ولكن إذا كانت السفرة مثل التي قمنا بها</u> العام الماضي فإن أثرها يمكن أن يكون أكبر.

نظَّمت (organized) لنا المدرسة رِحلة (trip/excursion) لُغويّة–سياحيّة (language-tourist) إلى تونس، قضينا أسبوعين في نشاطات (activities) مختلفة – المدينة والبحر والمحلات الشعبية والأسواق، وفي جميعها كان المدرسون يشجّعونا على التحدث إلى المواطنين؛ أحياناً يُجبرونا (force us) كما كان يفعل مستر وُدفيلد، والذي كان يتحدث مع الجميع <u>ولا يهمّه كيف تخرج الكلمات</u>، فقد كانت الصعوبة في اللَّهجَة المحليّة (dialect) تأتي بنتائج مضحكة ومسلّية جداً!

زُرنا مدرستين وتحدثنا إلى الطلاب، وشاركنا (participated) في تجربة في المختبر وفي إعداد مسرحية العيد. حتى النُزهات (outings) العادية علَّمتنا الكثير، <u>وبطريقة غير مباشرة</u>، قضينا فيها أوقاتاً ممتعة – لو قرأت كل يوم عن أي بلد ستعرف الكثير ولكن <u>التجربة العملية شيء آخر.</u>

أتصور أن مثل هذه السفرات العِلميّة (science trips) التي فيها زيارة إلى جبال أو سواحل أو أنهار، أو متاحف وآثار ومعارض، بحيث تتنوع النشاطات بين البحث في المواقع (sites) والمُحاضَرات (lectures) والنزهات، يمكن أن تعلم أكثر من فصل دراسي كامل – <u>ولكن مؤكد أن ذلك الفصل الدراسي كان ضعيفاً</u>!   (169 كلمة)

<u>Exercise 1</u> Explain how the underlined sentences and phrases helped in (a) giving a balanced opinion and (b) conveying images that can give a clearer idea of the Tunis trip.

<u>Exercise 2</u> Write a similar article from your own experience, perhaps by first drawing a mind-map. You may use the same points and details as shown in the piece above.

❖ After writing your articles, have them corrected by your teacher. Then rewrite them with the corrections and improvements, and keep them in your writing file.

غ.رسمية-**19** ما هو رأيك بالتبادل الطلابي؟ في **80-90** كلمة، تناول ما يلي، مع بيان الأسباب في آرائك:

هل هو مفيد، وكيف؟

هل تحب القيام به مع طالب عربي يستضيفك في بلده وأنت في بيتك هنا؟

ما المشاكل التي تتوقعها؟ وكيف يمكن تجنّبها أولاً وحلّها إذا حصلت هناك؟

INF-19: What is your opinion about student exchanges: are they beneficial? How? Would you like to do an exchange with an Arab student by hosting him in your home here and he hosts you in his country? What problems would you expect? And how could they be avoided in the first place and solved if they take place? In 80-90 words, write about this issue, by addressing the points above, and giving the reasons behind your views.

Let's start here by drawing a mind-map containing the ideas, giving some details.

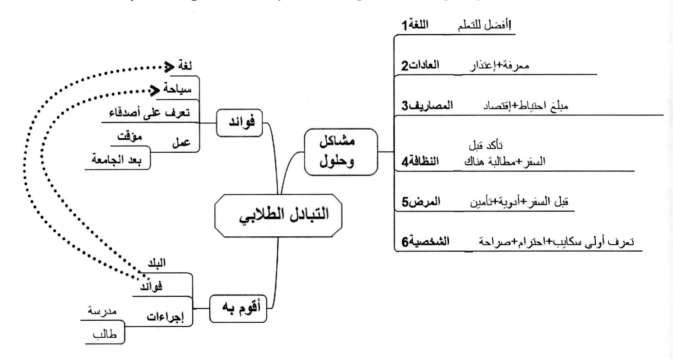

This mind-map allocates one branch for each of the first two parts of the task and one branch only for the remaining two tasks, since it makes sense to suggest the precaution and solution for each expected problem you mention. There is no estimated number of words for each branch, but you can allocate more or less words according to how many benefits or how many problems you list. This is not the major aspect - what you need to ensure is that you attend to all the parts of the task, without forgetting to support what you say with reasons.

Use this mind-map to write the article, but you should try to avoid writing the above details as they are, in bullet points or similar. Instead, write them in paragraphs of balanced sizes, with good structure benefiting from varied grammatical forms and the use of connecting words.

❖ After writing your article, have it corrected by your teacher. Then rewrite it with the corrections and improvements, and keep it in your writing file.

◾◾◾ FUTURE ASPIRATIONS, STUDY AND WORK ◾◾◾

غ.رسمية-**20** بعض الخريجين يرغبون في السفر مباشرة، يأخذون سنة توقف قبل الجامعة أو للعمل بعد الجامعة، وذلك من أجل الاطلاع إضافة إلى العمل، ولكن الأهل لا يعترضون إلى درجة جعل القضية مسألة حياة أو موت.

في حوالي **90-80** كلمة تناول هذا، بتضمين ما يلي:

(أ) إيجابيات وسلبيات السفر مباشرة بعد التخرج

(ب) كم هو مهم رأي الأهل ورغبتهم

(ت) أي حل وسط يرضي الطرفين.

INF-20 Some graduates like to travel as soon as they can, either as a gap year before university or to work after university or college, seeking, in addition to employment, to see the world, but their parents may object to the extent of making it a matter of life or death! In around 80-90 words, discuss this, including: (a) the pros and cons of travelling just after graduation, (b) how important the parents' opinions and wishes are, and (c) if there is any compromise that can satisfy both parties.

أهلي رقم **1**! أحب دائماً أن يكونوا راضين عني. لا يعني هذا أنني أتجاهَل (I ignore) طُموحي (my ambition) ورغبتي. فما العمل؟

إيجابيات السفر كثيرة، البعض يقول أنه مدرسة، ويأتي بخبرة (experience) في الحياة تنفع في الجامعة أو العمل. ولا تنس الفوائد المالية – هذا إذا حصلت على عمل؟ أحياناً يعاني (suffer) الشباب عند السفر، ويبدأون يحنّون (they long) لأيام الراحة في بيت الأهل.

أعرف شباباً صادفوا (they faced) المشاكل أول وصولهم: سرقت أموالهم أو جوازات السفر، مشاكل مع الشرطة، وقعوا ضحايا النَّصْب (victims of scam)... كانوا غير محظوظين (unfortunate).

غيرهم تغلّبوا على المصاعب (difficulties) الأولى، ثم نجحوا وقضوا وقتاً جميلاً بين الاطلاع والتعرف على أصدقاء جُدد والعمل وحتى البدء بالدراسة هناك. يعني تغيرت خططهم (their plans) التي قبل السفر.

عندما أنظر إلى هؤلاء وأولئك أجد أمرين:

"رأي" الأهل مهم جداً لأنهم أكثر معرفة بالحياة ولأنهم يحبونني ويخافون علي

"رغبة" الأهل أقل بكثير، ورغبتي مقدمة على رغبتهم وإلا يمكن أن أعيش بتَعاسة (in misery) طول العمر

وأنا أعمل في شيء لا أحبه... ولكن من يدري — ربما يتغير موقفي (my position) بعد ذلك.

فما العمل؟ إيجاد حل وسط، مثلاً السفر إلى بلد فيه أقارب أو أصدقاء يثق (trust) بهم الأهل، أو إلى مدينة في نفس بلدك وهذا يطمئن الأهل، أيضاً المشاكل أقل لأنه أقل بلدك.   (181 كلمة)

Exercise 1 Study the piece and see how the sentences with wavy underlines help to engage the reader and at the same time form a necessary part in fulfilling the requirements of the task, then (a) indicate any other sentences of the same sort, and (b) add or change anything that can improve the piece.

Exercise 2

(a) Who are هؤلاء وأولئك underlined with a single line?

(b) What is the grammar of the words in bold? ضحايا ، سرقت ، تنس

Exercise 3 How can the piece above be improved? Look into ways to make it more balanced:

(i)   in terms of how much is written for each part of the task (you may omit, add or replace words, phrases or full sentences),

(ii)   using other, perhaps better, connective words or fillers,

(iii) using other words or expressions that you think are better for the ideas and opinions given about this issue.

Exercise 4 Write (in around 80-90 words) a similar article, perhaps by first drawing a mind-map, and using, if you wish, similar ideas and detail to those in the suggested piece above, either:

(a) from your own experience, using your own discussion, ideas, opinions and suggestions

or

(b) by describing what questions and answers that you think your father and your brother are exchanging in their somewhat heated discussion about your brother's burning desire to go abroad in the gap year that he had already decided to take before starting his university course.

❖ After writing your articles, have them corrected by your teacher. Then rewrite them with the corrections and improvements, and keep them in your writing file.

غ.رسمية-21 (أ) ما هي خطط المستقبل فيما يَخص الدراسة بعد هذه المرحلة أو التدرّب على مهنة معينة؟

(ب) وكم تؤثر آراء الآخرين فيها؟ (ت) وهل توصّلت إلى قرار نهائي بشأنها أم لا تزال تبحث في الموضوع؟

تحدث عن ذلك في حوالي 80-90 كلمة.

INF-21 (a) What are your future plans concerning further education or training in a particular profession? **(b)** What effect do the opinions of others have? **(c)** Have you reached a final decision in this regards or are you still looking into the matter? Write about this in around 80-90 words.

Let's start here by drawing a mind-map containing the ideas, giving some details.

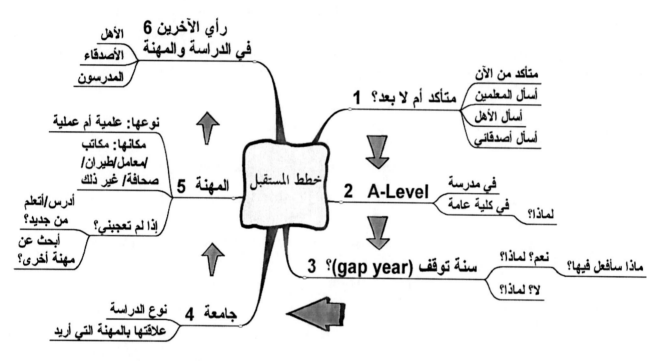

You can see that, in addition to branch numbers, this mind-map has got arrows which direct you through the right sequence of events in the coming years of your life. These arrows ensure that you follow this logical order when you write. That said, branch 6 can alternatively be included within the others in the form of a comment from a parent, a friend or teacher regarding your choice or desire.

Also, branch 5, which is about the profession, can be written about earlier, perhaps before branch 2. You can say that because you are committed to that profession, you will be going to this or that college, university etc.

Use this mind-map to write the article. Not all of the sub-branches are to be used, since some are alternatives to others.

You should try to avoid writing the above details as they are, in bullet points or similar. Instead, write them in paragraphs of balanced sizes, with good structure benefiting from varied grammatical forms and the use of connecting words.

❖ **After writing your article, have it corrected by your teacher. Then rewrite it with the corrections and improvements, and keep it in your writing file.**

غ.رسمية-22 أنت تقوم بأعمال تطوعية/ خيرية وتتحدث مع صديقك لتشجعه على ذلك. أكتب هذا، في نحو 80-90 كلمة، ذاكراً إن أحببت:

(أ) أنواع متعددة من العمل الخيري (ب) فوائد العمل الطوعي (ت) أمثلة من عملك أنت و/ أو آخرين في أعمال خيرية من أجل جعل اقتراحك جذاباً أكثر.

INF-22 You do volunteering/charity work and you are talking to your friend to encourage him to do the same. Write about that, in 80-90 words, mentioning: (a) different kinds of charity work, (b) the benefits of volunteering work, and (c) examples of what you and/or others are enjoying doing to make it more attractive.

يا عزيزي جواد، العمل الطَّوعي يختلف عن الوظيفي، ببساطة لأنك تشعر بالراحة وأنت تخدم الآخرين وليس لأجل الراتب. ثم أنت حُرّ تتركه كما تشاء، لا كالموظفين: يشكون من وظائفهم ولا يستطيعون تغييرها. لهذا، **لا تقرر** بسرعة، **لِنُجَرِّبْ التّطوّع** في أي عمل خَيري وسنرى ماذا تقول بعدها. سمى إبنة خالي تشكرني دائماً – تقول: لم **أتصور** أن حياتي يمكن أن تتغير تماماً، العمل الخيري جعلني أخدم الناس والمجتمع وأرضى عن نفسي، كلها دَفعةً واحدةً!

إذا تسألني ما أقترح عليك؟ أوه، جمعيتنا عندها العديد من البرامج. هل تحب مساعدة المرضى أم كبار السن؟ نشر التعليم أهم؟ ممكن. عندنا برنامج تعليم القراءة والكتابة لكبار السن، وحتى الصغار، لا تدري كم عدد الذين في سن المدرسة ولكن يتركونها للعمل لمساعدة عوائلهم – لا يعرفون حتى كتابة أسمائهم! ممكن تحب التعليم، فتعطي دروس تَقوية للطلاب – يعني مثل ما أفعل مع طلاب في الابتدائية والمتوسطة.

ولكن قُل لي: ألم تكُن تساعد **أبا** مرتضى في المطعم في العطل؟ **أخو** سمى يعمل في جمعية تقوم بتوزيع الطعام على المحتاجين، يمكنك التطوع للعمل يوم السبت أو الأحد – ما رأيك؟ (174 كلمة)

<u>Exercise 1</u> Study the piece and check how successful it was in satisfying the requirements of the. Use colour highlighting or another form of marking for quick future reference.

<u>Exercise 2</u> (a) Name the grammar topic that relates to the words in bold and explain the differences between the three: لم أتصور ، لنجرب ، لا تقرر .

(b) What is the grammar of the words in bold? أخو ، أبا

<u>Exercise 3</u> Write a similar article, keeping to 80-90 words, perhaps by first drawing a mind-map. You may use the same points and details as shown in the piece above.

❖ After writing your articles, have them corrected by your teacher. Then rewrite them with the corrections and improvements, and keep them in your writing file.

غ.رسمية-23 "العمل أثناء العطلة هو في الحقيقة قتل العطلة!" "كلا بكل تأكيد: إنه قتل الملل الذي يبدأ منذ الأسبوع الثاني من العطلة! العمل في العطلة هو مرح ونشاط ونقود – ماذا تريد أكثر من ذلك؟!"

ناقش هذه الآراء المتناقضة في حوالي 80-90 كلمة.

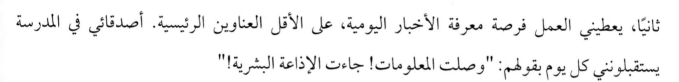

INF-23 'Working during the holidays is in effect killing the holidays!' 'Not at all: it is killing the boredom that starts from week 2 of the holidays! Holiday work means fun, activity and money – what do you want more?!' Discuss, in around 80-90 words, these conflicting opinions.

هناك عدة إمكانيات للكتابة في هذا الموضوع، منها:

(أولاً) <u>عمل بدوام جُزئي</u>

إنتهت سنة وأنا أوزّع الجرائد على البيوت في شارعنا والشوارع القريبة. البعض يتصور أنه عمل ممل لكن لا أراه هكذا. أولاً، أستيقظ مبكرًا، فأصلي صلاة الفجر في وقتها، ثم المشي والنشاط قبل المدرسة.

ثانيًا، يعطيني العمل فرصة معرفة الأخبار اليومية، على الأقل العناوين الرئيسية. أصدقائي في المدرسة يستقبلونني كل يوم بقولهم: "وصلت المعلومات! جاءت الإذاعة البشرية!"

ثالثًا، أحصل من صاحب محل الجرائد على أجر (wages) لا بأس به، وهذا يساعدني على شراء الأشياء التي لا يستطيع غيري شراءها لأن مصروف الجيب لا يكفي. (82 كلمة)

(ثانيًا) <u>عمل بدوام جزئي في العطلة</u>

لا أحب العمل في المحلات الكبيرة، ولكن ماذا أفعل وهو العمل الوحيد المتوفر في منطقتنا؟ إنه عمل مُرهِق جدًّا (very exhausting) – أنقل الصناديق والأغراض (things) المعروضة للبيع وجميع المطلوب مني طِيلة السبت والأحد ...

وعندما عملت في قسم الأطعمة الجاهزة، شبعت من رائحة الطعام، حتى صرت لا أحبه أبدًا!

ولكن هناك بعض الأمور الجيدة، فبعض العاملين طيّبون، وصارت لي صداقات معهم.

وطبعًا هناك الأجر الذي أتقاضاه (I get)، وهو السبب في عملي هناك.

ولا أنسى الفرصة الكبيرة لأمي كي توصيني بشراء ما تحتاجه، طبعاً بأرخص الأسعار!   (81 كلمة)

(ثالثًا) <u>عمل بدوام كامل في العطلة</u>

كانت العطلة الصيفية أحلى عطلة قضيتها في حياتي، لا لأني سافرت إلى بلد عربي، ولكن لأني اشتغلت في نادي الرياضة.

كنت أقوم بعدة أعمال وأقدم خدمات (services) مختلفة للأعضاء (members) والزُّوّار (guests)، وهذا ما أحبه. هذا إضافة إلى قيامي بممارسة تمارين الأثقال والسباحة.

كان كثير من العاملين بعمري، لذلك قضينا أوقاتاً جميلة جدًا، وكانت لنا مواقف مضحكة.

حصلت على أجر جيد جدًّا، وكان مصروفي (my expenses) قليلاً لأني كنت أعمل أكثر الوقت، فقد أدَّخَرت (I save) كلفة الإيجار (rent) إلى آخر العطلة، وشراء بعض الحاجيات قبل المدرسة.   (79 كلمة)

<u>Exercise 1</u> Give the full grammar of the sentences in bold:

. كان كثير من العاملين بعمري , إنه عمل مُرهِق جدًّا , لا يستطيع غيري شراءها

<u>Exercise 2</u> Try to combine piece no. 1 with either piece 2 or piece 3 to give an account of work in both school time and the holidays, but do not exceed 120 words.

<u>Exercise 3</u> Write (in around 80-90 words) a similar article, perhaps by first drawing a mind-map, and using, if you wish, similar ideas and detail to those in the suggested piece above, either:
(a) from your own experience, using your own discussion, ideas, opinions and suggestions
or
(b) by using one or more of the photos above for inspiration.

❖ After writing your articles, have them corrected by your teacher. Then rewrite them with the corrections and improvements, and keep them in your writing file.

غ.رسمية-24 في حوالي 80-90 كلمة، أكتب عن:

موضوع الوظائف والمهن مستخدماً ما يعمل فيه بعض من تعرف من أفراد عائلتك أو الأصدقاء، و/ أو ما تحب أن تعمل في مجاله في المستقبل.

INF-24 In around 80-90 words, write about the topic of careers and professions, using what some members of your family or their friends do, and/or the field you wish to work in in the future.

The task doesn't ask for specific details to be included, therefore you should include all the main relevant ones. It also gives you the freedom to write in one of three possible ways: other people, or your ambitions for the future, or both.

If you like, you can use some of the following phrases as starters or to give you ideas for writing about this using the two alternatives: careers and jobs in your family or people that you know, or your own aspirations in this regard.

Also, the following (incomplete) list of relevant words - careers, job description and salaries - should prove helpful.

يمكن الكتابة في هذا الموضوع بعدة طرق، منها:

(أولاً) عمل أو مهنة أفراد عائلتك أو غيرهم ممن تعرف

الوظائف الحكومية مضمونة (guaranteed) من ناحيتي ...

لهذا فإن والدي يعمل موظّفاً (employee) في وزارة الإسكان، رغم أن عدة شركات ...

أما أخي سلام، فإن مُؤَهّله (his qualification) في ...

جارتنا منال وجدت أن أفضل طريقة للجمع بين واجبات عائلتها والعمل هو أن تعمل من البيت موظفةَ تسويق (marketing) على الانترنت...

(ثانيًا) العمل أو المهنة التي تفكر فيها لنفسك في المستقبل

أهم شيء في الوظيفة فُرَصَ التَّرقِيَةِ (promotion prospects)، وإلا ...

لا مانع (no objection) من العمل من التاسعة إلى الخامسة (nine to five)، ولكن بشرط (on the condition/provided)...

أحب مهنة التدريب الرياضي، فإنها ...

ما أروعَ مهنة مُصَفِّفَة الشّعر (hairdresser)! عمل ودردشة وأخبار المجتمع، ولكن الدوام ...

أعرف ما أريد: طبيبة في عِيادَتي الخاصة (my private clinic)، فإني ...

لَن أكون إلاّ صحفياً (journalist)! هذا الذي ...

بعض الوظائف/ الأعمال/ المِهَن (jobs/careers/professions): بائع (salesman) ، مُذيع (news reader) ، مُبَرمِج (programmer) ، فَنّي (technician) ، مُتَرجِم (translator/interpreter) ، مدرس/ معلم (teacher) ، محامي (lawyer) ، رجل/ إمرأة أعمال (businessman/business woman) ، فنان (artist) ، ضابط/ ضابطة جيش/ شرطة (army/police officer) ، مُمَرِّض (nurse) ، صيدلي (pharmacist) ، مهندس (engineer) ، ميكانيكي (mechanic) ، كهربائي (electrician) ، سَبّاك (plumber) ، مُصوّر (photographer)

وصف العمل: مُشَوِّق (interesting) ، مُتَنَوِّع (varied) ، مُتعِب (tiring) ، مُمِلّ (boring) ، مُجْهِد (stressful)

الأجْر/ الرّاتب (wages/salary): جَيِّد/ مُجْزٍ (well paid) ، غير جَيِّد/ غير مُجْزٍ/ قليل (underpaid)

You don't need to write the starters - if you are going to use them - in the sequence shown or even in separate paragraphs. Write them in one or more paragraphs and in whatever sequence you like to produce a good, coherent presentation of your ideas.

See how the words with <u>wavy underlines</u> give either (i) the reasons behind the career choice (whether objective or out of desire/love) (ما أروع, أحب, أهم شيء, أفضل طريقة, مؤهله), or (ii) how the person is quite determined in what they want (لن أكون إلا, أعرف ما أريد), or (iii) just the start of the process of expanding on the starter (لكن بشرط, رغم أن, من ناحيتي).

➤ Write your answer to the task by <u>choosing only one of the two parts of the suggestion</u>.

<u>Exercise 1</u> Now try <u>to combine both suggestions</u> to come up with a piece that describes your future career ambitions along with the careers and jobs of others that might have influenced your decision. Do not exceed 120 words.

<u>Exercise 2</u>

(a) What is the grammar of each of the following words in bold? موظفةَ ، موظفاً

(b) Give the grammar of the words in bold: عائلتها ، مؤهله .

(c) What is the grammar topic of each of the words in bold? إلا صحفياً ، ما أروع ، لا مانع

<u>Exercise 3</u> Write, in 80-90 words, a similar article from your own experience. You may use the same points and details as shown in the suggested piece above, but it is better to use other careers and professions, from the suggested list or otherwise.

❖ After writing your articles, have them corrected by your teacher. Then rewrite them with the corrections and improvements, and keep them in your writing file.

▮▮▮▮▮▮ INTERNATIONAL AND GLOBAL DIMENSION ▮▮▮▮▮▮

غ.رسمية-25 أكتب، في 80-90 كلمة، عن مناسبة أو مباراة رياضية حضرتها أو شاهدتها من التلفاز، ذاكراً:

(أ) الحدث والمكان (ب) وصف الملعب (ت) بعض لمحات من المباراة (ث) مشاعرك.

INF-25 Write, in around 80-90 words, about a sports event or match that you have watched in a stadium or on TV, mentioning: (a) the event and place, (b) details of the stadium or pitch, (c) the match itself, and (d) your feelings.

أحب لعبة التنس منذ الصّغر (childhood)، ولكن لم يتحقق لي حلم مشاهدة مباراة في بطولة ومبلدون ومبلدون للتنس إلا العام الماضي.

الملعب الأخضر، وسط ومبلدون الخضراء، واحدة من أجمل مناطق لندن، كان جميلاً، ولم تمطر السماء وتعطّل المباراة. الملعب مليء بالمتفرجين، خصوصاً وأن المباراة كانت بين بطلين كبيرين. جلست – بين أبي وأختي وأخي – لا أصدق أني هناك!

قعدنا (we sat) في صفّ عالٍ من المقاعد. صحيح أننا نرى **اللاعبين** أبعد من متفرجي الصفوف السفلى ولكنه أفضل في مشاهدة الملعب كله وحركات **اللاعبين** وكل شيء. كما كان هناك شاشة كبيرة تعرض النقاط التي يسجلها **اللاعبان**، إضافة إلى شاشة تلفزيون كبيرة تعرض المباراة كما تشاهدها لو كنت في البيت. يعني كانت المشاهدة متكاملة (comprehensive).

كانت المباراة قوية، فيها الكثير من اللعب المستمر طويلاً (long rallies) مع الحركات البهلوانية (acrobatic) والضربات التي يُخدع (fools) بها كل منهما الآخر – شيء جميل جداً.

أكيد أنني لن أنسى ذلك اليوم، ولكن أريد أن أتذكره بالصور، لهذا أخذت صوراً كثيرة للمباراة وللملعب والأهل، وطبعاً لي شخصياً (selfie)!   (150 كلمة)

Exercise 1 Study the above piece and check how successful it was in satisfying the requirements of the task.

Exercise 2 Explain the grammar of the words in bold: اللاعبان ، اللاعبين ، اللاعبين .

Exercise 3 Write a similar article from your own experience, perhaps by first drawing a mind-map. You may use the same points and details as shown in the suggested piece above.

❖ After writing your articles, have them corrected by your teacher. Then rewrite them with the corrections and improvements, and keep them in your writing file.

غ.رسمية-**26** في حوالي 90-80 كلمة،

(أ) صِفي عَرضاً رئيسياً حضرته أو شاهدته على التلفاز،

مضيفةً (ب) كيف تفاعل الجمهور، و (ت) كيف أحسست أنت،

(ث) فيها إذا سترغبين في الذهاب إلى حدث مشابه في المستقبل ولماذا.

INF-26 (a) Describe, in around 80-90 words, a major performance which you attended or saw on TV, including, in addition, (b) how the audience reacted, (c) how you felt, and (d) whether you would like to go to a similar event in the future and why.

Let's start here by drawing a mind-map containing the ideas, giving some details.

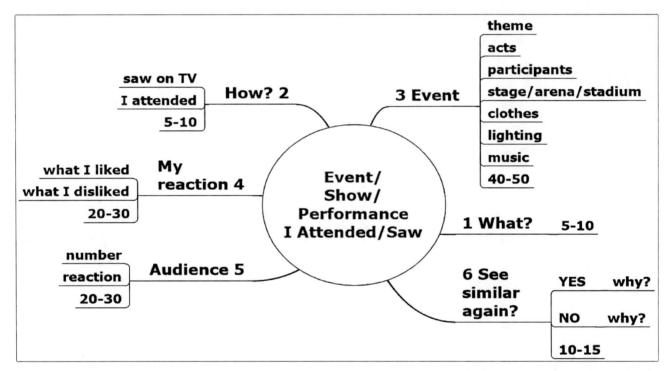

You can see that this mind-map contains all the features, including the number of words for each branch. And you would perhaps agree that for such a task the main paragraph should be the one that describes the event itself, i.e. branch 3. But you should never overlook the rest of the writing task, which is the audience reaction, your reaction, why etc.

If you like, you can use <u>some</u> of the following paragraphs and sentences as starters or to give you ideas for writing on the performance which you saw.

حضرت عرض "أليغريا" لفرقة "سيرك دي سوليه" الكندية في إبن بطوطة مول في مدينة دبي، وذلك في عطلة الربيع.

كنا أربعة أشخاص: أنا و...

العرض حول موضوع ...

والفرقة لا تستخدم السّتائر (curtains) عند تغيير الديكور، ولكن الممثلين هم الذين يأتون بالأثاث اللازم ثم

يُخرِجونه! وقد أعجبني هذا لأنه ...

كان ديكور المسرح رائعاً، بل إن المسرح كله داخل خيمة كبيرة جداً أقاموها (they erected) لأجل العرض.

أما الإضاءة فاستخدمت أنواراً غامقة (dark)، وهذه ...

ولكن ملابس الممثلين ...

أما الموسيقى فكانت ...

التمثيل بحركات الأكروباتيك وبعض حركات السّيرك (circus)

الذي نعرفه كان رائعاً، خصوصاً ...

ومن أكثر ما أضحكني هو دور المُهَرّج (clown) فإنه قام بـ ...

إلا أن أمي قالت بأنه لم تعجبها فقرة ... بسبب ...

كان رد فعل (reaction) الجُمهور/ الحُضُور (audience)، وهم أكثر من ألفين، حَماسيّاً حتى أن بعضهم ...

أستطيع أن أقول أني أحب وأتمنى أن أشاهد الأعمال القادمة لهذه الفرقة لأنها نجحت في ...

كما أن الفرقة تقوم بمساعدة الفقراء مباشرةً، أيضاً بتشغيلهم لتحضير ملابس ومواد العُروض.

Exercise 1 Use the mind-map above to write the article from your own experience. You should try to avoid writing the above details as they are, in bullet points or similar. Instead, write them in paragraphs of balanced sizes, with good structure benefiting from varied grammatical forms and the use of connecting words. Pay attention also to your punctuation and handwriting.

Exercise 2 Complete the piece describing the Cirque du Soleil show 'Alegria', concentrating on adding the details that complete the piece (regardless of the number of words you end up with.)

Exercise 3 Try to condense the piece you complete in Exercise 2 to around 100 words.

Exercise 4 Write, in 80-90 words, a similar article from your own experience. You may use the same points and details as shown in the suggested piece above

❖ After writing your articles, have them corrected by your teacher. Then rewrite them with the corrections and improvements, and keep them in your writing file.

غ.رسمية-27 هل للمحافظة على "المصادر الطبيعية" علاقة بما يسمى "المعيشة الخضراء"؟ بيّني ذلك من خلال محادثة مع صديقتك تشجعينها فيها على التعامل الصحيح مع المصادر الطبيعية، تتضمن:

(أ) تعريف كل منهما   (ب) المشكلة الحالية في استخدام المصادر الطبيعية لكوكب الأرض

(ت) كيف تؤثر المعيشة الخضراء على المصادر الطبيعية.

أكتبي حوالي 80-90 كلمة.

INF-27 Is preserving 'natural resources' related to what is called 'green living'? Explain this through a conversation with your friend in which you encourage her to deal in the correct way with the natural resources, including: (a) a definition of each of the two, (b) current problems concerning the use of the Earth's natural resources, and (c) how green living affects natural resources. Write around 80-90 words.

لست مجنونة بالبيئة! قصدي أريدك فقط أن لا تؤذي نفسك، لأن إيذاء الأرض سيؤثر علينا جميعاً. أكيد جرّبت الحال عندما ينقطع الماء – نتيجة التبذير (reckless consumption) في الاستخدام شِحَّة (scarcity) مياه الشرب والغسيل وسيقطع الماء من المحطة.

المعيشة الخضراء ليست موضة تعجبنا، حتى ولا تصرف جميل منّا – إنها العيش بشكل مسؤول (responsible) يراقب استخدام الماء والكهرباء ويدعم شراء الحاجيات التي أُنتِجَت (produced) بشكل لا يضر بكوكب الأرض. هذا ضروري للمستقبل، لأننا عندما نقتصد (economise) في استخدام الماء والكهرباء، فإننا نحافظ على المصادر الطبيعية للأرض للأجيال القادمة (future generations).

بدلاً من حرق الوقود والغابات يمكن توليد الكهرباء من أشعة الشمس والرّياح. طبعاً سنستخدم المصادر الطبيعية التي أقصدها، ولكنها تُعوّض (are compensated) بالتدوير. لماذا ترمين كل شيء في الزبالة؟ لماذا لا تأخذينها إلى حاويات التدوير (recycling containers) وسيقومون بإعادة إنتاجها بدلاً من مصادر طبيعية جديدة؟

وهناك فائدة إضافية (bonus): المعيشة الخضراء تعني أيضاً تقليل التلوّث (pollution) بأنواعه – بالاهتمام بما تأكلين وما تلبسين وغير ذلك، وهو ما سيقلل من هَدر (wasting) المصادر الطبيعية...

أحب أن تكوني إنسانة مسؤولة، وهذا ليس غريباً على إحساسك بالآخرين وحبك لهم.   (158 كلمة)

<u>Exercise 1</u> Study the piece above and check how successful it was in satisfying the requirements of the task by determining which paragraphs or sentences relate to which part of the task. Use colour highlighting or another form of marking for quick future reference (different underlining styles are used to highlight connective words, fillers and effective expressions).

<u>Exercise 2</u> How effective/persuasive are the arguments presented? How can they be improved, perhaps through:

(i) making them more balanced in terms of how much is written for each part of the task (you may omit, add or replace words, phrases or full sentences),

(ii) using other, perhaps better, connective words or fillers,

(iii) using other words or expressions that you think are better for the ideas and suggestions in this important contemporary issue?

<u>Exercise 3</u>

(a) What is the grammar of the verbs in bold?

(b) How do you write the expression they effect in another form? تعوض ، أنتجت ، يقطع

<u>Exercise 4</u> Write (in around 80-90 words) a similar article, perhaps by first drawing a mind-map, and using, if you wish, similar ideas and detail to those in the suggested piece above, either:

(a) from your own experience, using your own discussion, ideas, opinions and suggestions

or

(b) by talking about the young people in the photo - what they are doing, why you think they are doing that, whether they seem to be enjoying it or just doing it out of a sense of duty, and whether you would like to join if you were invited to do so and why.

❖ After writing your articles, have them corrected by your teacher. Then rewrite them with the corrections and improvements, and keep them in your writing file.

الكتابة بأسلوب رسمي

Formal Writing

Length: 130-150 words

This is only 'recommended', i.e. a guideline, and 'Students will not be penalised for writing more or fewer words than recommended in the word count or for going beyond the mandatory bullets.'

Options: Two options; students must answer one only.

Type of writing: Formal register (or style).

Topics: The Specification Themes (and their sub-themes) of the Edexcel 2017 GCSE Specification.

Assessment: The question 'assesses students on their ability to convey information, narrate, express and justify ideas and opinions, and interest or convince the reader.'

IMPORTANT: Please refer to the Edexcel 2017 Specification for a detailed description of how marks are awarded for this question.

IDENTITY AND CULTURE

رسمية-1 أكتب 130-150 كلمة حول ما يلي:

(أ) هل توافق على أن الشباب يتعايشون مع الشباب من بلدان وأديان وخلفيّات أخرى في حين أن آباءهم يفشلون في ذلك في نفس المجتمع متعدد الثقافات الذي يعيشون فيه؟

إذا كنت توافق أو لا توافق (ب) وضح الأسباب؛

(ت) كيف يمكن تشجيع الناس على النظر إلى الآخرين الذين يصفونهم بالـ "آخرين"؟ بشكل صحيح/ إنساني

FR-1 (a) Do you agree that young people get on very well with young people from different countries, religions and backgrounds while their parents fail to do so in the same multicultural society they live in? If you agree or disagree, (b) explain why; also (c) how can people be encouraged to look in a healthier way upon those whom they label 'others'? Write 130-150 words.

لأني أعيش في مجتمع متعدّد الثّقافات هو المجتمع البريطاني فإني أوافق تماماً على أن الشباب يمكنهم التّعايُش (co-existence) أفضل بكثير من آبائهم وأمهاتهم مع "الآخرين" من أتباع الدّيانات الأخرى أو القادمين من بلاد تختلف في الدين أو اللغة أو الثقافة.

هناك أكثر من سبب لذلك:

أولاً– نشأة (upbringing) الأب والأم في مجتمع غير متنوّع، فيجهلان كيفية التعامل مع الآخرين.

ثانياً– الجهل بالآخرين وطريقتهم في الحياة والحكم عليها أنها خطأ أو حرام أو عَيب.

ثالثاً– وجود مشاكل بين البلدان الأصلية أدّت إلى الكراهية.

أما الشباب فقد نشؤوا مع أولاد "الآخرين" وبناتهم فصاروا ليسوا "آخرين" بل شباباً مثلهم في نفس المجتمع ونفس المدارس ويذهبون إلى نفس النوادي والملاعب وعندهم نفس المشاكل والطّموحات (ambitions)، وسيعملون في نفس الأماكن. عندما يرى صديقه يدخل في مسجد أو كنيسة أو معبد (temple) يقول أنه ذاهب لحضور الصلاة كما يفعل هو، فحتى لو كان يتبع ديناً آخر فإنه لا يؤثر على علاقته به وتعامله الإنساني (humane) معه. هم يعلمون أن المجتمع ينتظر من الجميع أن يتعاونوا لأجل الجميع، وأن الأفكار السلبية تعرّض المجتمع للمشاكل وهم سيفشلون.

أهم نقطة يجب توضيحها للكبار: المشاكل لا تحلّها الكراهية والجهل؛ وحتى إن كانت المشاعر السلبية في القلوب فعليهم منعها من التأثير على التعامل الطيب الذي يجمع بين حسن الأخلاق ورعاية مصالح (interests) الفرد والمجتمع. إذا كان الإنسان متديّناً (religious) فذلك يجعله ينظر إلى الناس كلهم كما جاء في الحديث الشريف: ((خَيرُ النّاس مَنْ نَفَعَ النّاس)).   (217 كلمة)

Exercise 1 Study the piece above and check how successful it was in satisfying the requirements of the task by determining which paragraphs or sentences relate to which part of the task. Use colour highlighting or another form of marking for quick future reference.

Exercise 2 Translate the underlined words: الدين أو اللغة أو الثقافة ، خطأ أو حرام أو عَيب .

Exercise 3 What grammatical position does each of the words in bold have?

وجود مشاكل ، أهم نقطة

Exercise 4 How can the piece above be improved? Look into ways to make it more balanced:
(i)   in terms of how much is written for each part of the task (you may omit, add or replace words, phrases or full sentences),
(ii) using other, perhaps better, connective words or fillers,
(iii) using other words or expressions that you think are better for the ideas given about this important issue.

Exercise 5 Try to condense this piece, to reduce it to around 130-150 words, while preserving the main points.

Exercise 6 Write (in around 130-150 words) a similar article, perhaps by first drawing a mind-map, and using, if you wish, similar ideas to those in the suggested piece above, either:

(a) from your own experience, using your own discussion, ideas, opinions and suggestions
or
(b) by responding to this photo, to describe what can be extracted from it with regards to this issue.

❖ After writing your articles, have them corrected by your teacher. Then rewrite them with the corrections and improvements, and keep them in your writing file.

رسمية-2 صِفي، في 130-150 كلمة، أفراد عائلتك وصديقاتك الـمُقَرَّبات:

(أ) سِماتهم/ صفاتهم العقلية والشخصية (ب) إهتماماتهم (ت) العلاقات فيما بينهم

(ث) تأثير ذلك كله على علاقتك بهم، ولماذا.

FR-2 Describe, in 130-150 words, your family and close friends: (a) their mental and personality characteristics, (b) the relationships between them, (c) their interests, and also (d) how does all of this affect your relationship with them?

Let's start here by drawing a mind-map containing the ideas, giving some details.

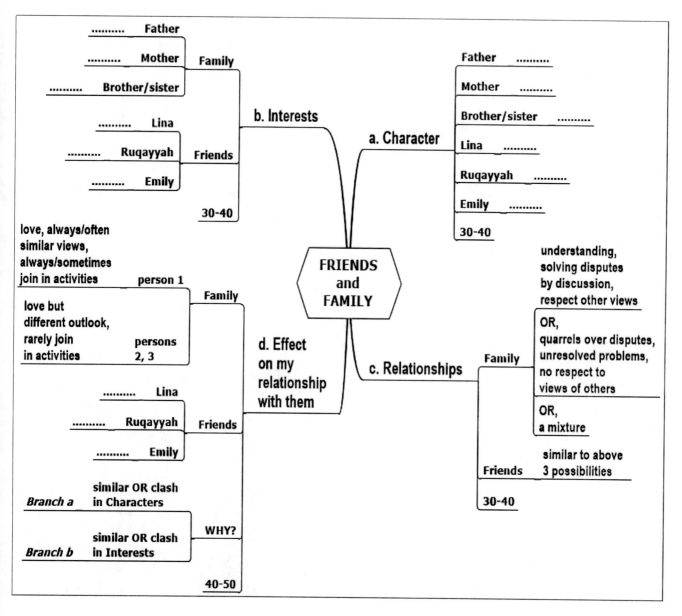

You can see that this mind-map does not specify the characteristics and interests; the same with the friends part of branch d. This is deliberate, to encourage you to use the characteristics and interests you want, whether they are what you experience in real life or imaginary, and then to change branch c and change and complete branch d according to what you expect from the different characteristics and interests that these people in your life have.

Protected by copyright. No page may be photocopied except for the user's own use.

You can use the following vocabulary lists for characteristics and interests:

to care for/to look after إعْتَنى بِـ	selfish أنانيّ	intelligent ذَكِيّ
to pick on لامَ	untidy غَيْر مُرَتَّب	serious جادّ
to chat/chatter دَرْدش/ ثَرْثَر	annoying مُزْعِج	comfortable/at ease مُريح/ سَهل
to annoy أزْعَج	crazy مَجْنون	gentle رَقِيق
to quarrel تَشاجَرَ	depressed مُكْتَئِب	cheerful مُبْتَهِج / مَرِح
to argue جادَل	bossy مُتَسَلِّط	reliable مَوْثوق /يُعتمَد عليه
to rely on وَثِقَ بِـ	chatty ثَرْثار	understanding مُتَفَهِّم

doing sports ممارسة الرياضة	cooking الطَّبْخ	reading القِراءة/ المُطالَعَة
photography التَّصوير الفُوتوغرافي	watching TV مُشاهَدة التِّلْفاز	reading stories قراءة القصص
التَّنَزُّه في الحديقة العامّة/ شاطئ البحر	films and plays الأفلام والمسرحيات	music الموسيقى
walking in the park/along the beach	theatre/museums المَسرَح/ المَتاحِف	surfing the net تَصَفُّح الانترَنَت
Do-it-yourself/DIY إعمَل بنفسِك	gardening العَمَل في الحديقة	drawing الرَّسْم

Try to explain why you describe someone with a certain characteristic by using a short sentence or even a longer sentence that tells of patterns of behaviour. For example, if you say that person 1 is 'selfish' you can explain this by saying 'she only thinks of herself', or by saying 'she always goes up without helping to clear the table and wash the dishes with us', and so on.

In addition, you can attend to the four parts of the task in any manner, mixing branches a and b and/or mixing branches c and d, or otherwise.

Use this mind-map to write the article. Decide how many words each of these four branches needs, perhaps by looking at how many each sub-branch needs. The suggested number of words in the above mind-map is for a balanced response to the task; otherwise you can write the number of words that is required for what you want to write.

You should try to avoid writing the above details as they are, in bullet points or similar. Instead, write them in paragraphs of balanced sizes, with good structure benefiting from varied grammatical forms and the use of connecting words.

Exercise Using other characteristics and interests of your friends and family and other elements of the task, write a similar article in around 130-150 words.

❖ **After writing your articles, have them corrected by your teacher. Then rewrite them with the corrections and improvements, and keep them in your writing file.**

رسمية-3 "القدوة ذات أهمية فائقة". أكتب 130-150 كلمة للتعبير عن رأيك بخصوص هذه المقولة حول:

(أ) أثر القدوة على الأفراد   (ب) أثرها على المجتمع

(ت) أمثلة لأشخاص يمثلون قدوة لك وللمجتمع أثّروا في نظرتك إلى الحياة أو تصرفاتك تجاه الآخرين.

FR-3 'Role models are extremely important.' Write 130-150 words to express your opinion regarding this statement on (a) the effect of role models on individuals, (b) on society, (c) example(s) of a role model (or role models) who has (have) influenced your outlook on life or your behaviour towards others.

If you like, you can use some of the following paragraphs and sentences as starters or to give you ideas for writing this article.

أوّلاً وقبلَ كُلّ شيء، ليس من الضروري أن تكون القدوة شخصية مشهورة، فإني ...

أنا شخصياً، أثّرت في شخصية عمّي ...

لا شكّ في أن المَشاهير (celebrities) يمكن أن يكونوا قدوة حسنة، ولكن يمكن ...

وبِناءً عليه (therefore)، من المهم أن لا نقلد أي شخصية مشهورة ...

مثلاً لاعب كرة قدم مشهور يمكن أن ينفع ...

كما يمكن أن يضرّ، لأن الشباب ينبهرون (become dazzled) ...

وقد وجدت أن شخصية جراح القلب مجدي يعقوب* تمثل قدوة في جوانب متعددة ...

كما وجدت أن شخصية الرياضي محمد فرح* قدوة حسنة، لأنه عادةً ...

أما شخصية المعمارية زها حديد*، فإنها قدوة ...

(٭ هذه الشخصيات الثلاث موجودة في كتابي "صديقك العربي" لمنهاج جي سي أس إي 2017.)

As you can see, you don't need to attend to the points of the task according to their sequence in the question; you can mix them as you go along with the piece. But make sure that all points are included.

Three individuals who achieved world fame are mentioned above as each of them can be a positive role model to certain sectors of society as well as to society as a whole. You do not need to include more than one role model in your answer, but variety can support your answer especially if you don't find much to say about only one celebrity.

Don't overlook your punctuation and handwriting.

❖ After writing your article, have it corrected by your teacher. Then rewrite it with the corrections and improvements, and keep it in your writing file.

رسمية-4 في 130-150 كلمة، أكتب عن عادات الطعام والتمارين الرياضية في عائلتك:

(أ) ما نوع الطعام/ الأطعمة من مناطق أخرى من العالم يفضلونها

(ب) هل التمارين الرياضية مهمة كالطعام أم هي مهملة

(ت) هل هناك "مجنون" تمارين أو متطرف تغذية

(ث) كيف يمكن تشجيع من يهمل هذين الجانبين على الاهتمام بهما.

FR-4 In 130-150 words, write a report on the exercise and diet habits of your family: (a) what sort of food/cuisine(s) is/are preferred, (b) whether exercise is as important as food or is otherwise neglected, (c) if there is any exercise-crazy or diet fanatic in the family; also (d) how you encourage those who overlook these two areas not to ignore them.

Let's start here by drawing a mind-map containing the ideas, giving some details.

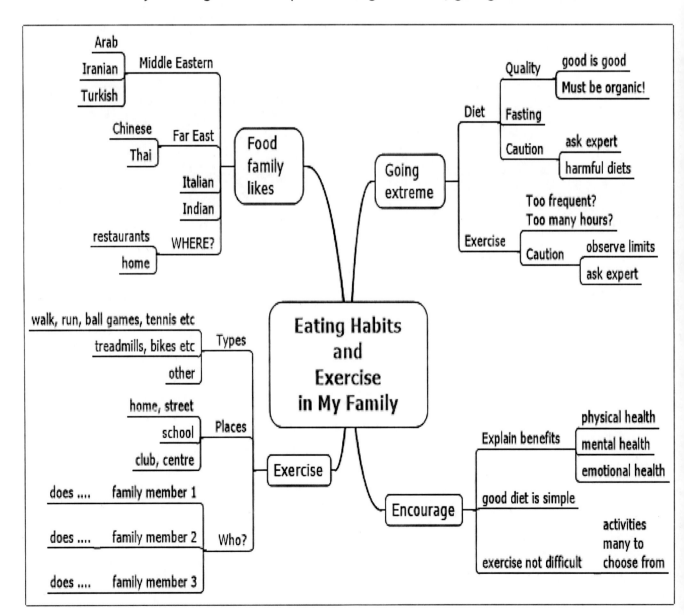

Use this mind-map to write the article. Decide first the order, which is rather straightforward for this mind-map: either eating habits first followed by exercise, or vice versa, then the 'going extreme' branch with its caution sub-branch, ending with your ideas of how to encourage members of your family not to ignore these two areas. Then, decide how many words each of these four branches needs, perhaps by looking at how many each sub-branch needs. Some 40-50 words for each of the two main branches and 25-40 for the other two seem appropriate.

Obviously, you could have incorporated the 'encouragement' part in each of the two main parts to end up with a slightly different structure, so be flexible!

You should try to avoid writing the above details as they are, in bullet points or similar. Instead, write them in paragraphs of balanced sizes, with good structure benefiting from varied grammatical forms and the use of connecting words.

Pay attention also to your punctuation and handwriting.

Exercise Would you like to join these people in their exercise session? And why? What might attract you and what might discourage you from exercise as a whole when you see such photos? And why? Write 130-150 words in response to this, supporting your argument with personal experience or otherwise.

❖ After writing your articles, have them corrected by your teacher. Then rewrite them with the corrections and improvements, and keep them in your writing file.

رسمية-5 "بوجود مختلف البرامج على شبكة الانترنت لا حاجة إلى التلفزيون وبرامجه المملّة وأخباره المزعجة

ومسلسلاته المكرّرة".

(أ) ناقش هذا الرأي: كم هو صادق

(ب) هل هناك من يقول به فعلاً

(ت) هل رأيهم هذا مبرر

(ث) وإذا كان ذلك كذلك، هل أننا نشهد بداية نهاية التلفزيون؟

أكتب 130-150 كلمة.

FR-5 'With the different programmes on the internet there is no need for the TV and its boring programmes, troubling news and repeated soaps.' (a) Discuss this opinion: how true is it, (b) are there actually people saying this, (c) is their opinion justified, and (d) if that is so, are we witnessing the beginning of the end of TV? Write 130-150 words.

لا شكّ في أن الشبكة العالمية (internet) دخلت في جميع المجالات ومنها التلفزيون. ويقوم المُبَرمِجون (programmers) بكتابة برامج تجعل من الحاسوب والانترنت أمراً جَذّاباً (attractive) حتى لكبار السّنّ.

برامج التلفزيون أوقاتها غالباً ما تكون مُحَدَّدة (set/fixed)، بينما موادّ الانترنت تدخل إليها متى ما تشاء. صحيح يمكن تسجيل (record) برنامج أو فيلم التلفزيون لتشاهده لاحقاً (later)، لكنك تستطيع مشاهدة الفيلم/ البرنامج من الانترنت على أية حال، أيضاً تنزيله (download) وحفظه (save it) في مِلَفّ (file) كي تشاهده حتى ولو انقطع الانترنت. بل يمكن أن يشاهده صديقك بعد أن يستلمه أو رابطه (its link) منك بلَمْح البَصَر (in no time)!

إضافة إلى الوقت، أقوم بتنزيل الأفلام الوَثائقيّة (documentaries) والبوليسيّة (thrillers) التي تُعجِبُني أنا، لا مسؤولي برامج التلفزيون الذين لهم ذَوق (taste) مختلف.

حتى الأخبار، فإن الشباب صاروا يجدون في المُدَوَّنات (blogs) والمُنتَدَيات (forums) وسيلة أفضل لمعرفة الأخبار من مواقع تفكّر بالطريقة التي تناسبهم. هذا غير البرامج التّفاعُليّة (interactive) كغرف الحِوار (chat rooms) أو برامج التسلية والتعليم غير الموجودة في التلفزيون.

لذا، فإني أرى أن الكثيرين يؤمنون بهذه الفكرة. <u>ولكني</u> لا أظنّ أن نهاية التلفزيون بدأت، لأن الكثيرين من الكبار لا يزالون يحبون برامجه، والجلوس في جوّ عائلي غير موجود أمام الحاسوب، ولأنه لا يزال يقدم ما هو غير موجود على الانترنت. (175 كلمة)

<u>Exercise 1</u> Study the piece above and check how successful it was in satisfying the requirements of the task by determining which paragraphs or sentences relate to which part of the task. Use colour highlighting or another form of marking for quick future reference (underlining is used to highlight connective words, fillers and useful words).

<u>Exercise 2</u> Name the grammar topic that relates to the words in bold:

أن يشاهده ، كي تشاهده ، لتشاهده.

<u>Exercise 3</u> Translate the following underlined words: لا شك في ، غالباً ما تكون ، حتى ولو .

<u>Exercise 4</u> How can the piece above be improved? Look into ways to make it more balanced:

(iv) in terms of how much is written for each part of the task (you may omit, add or replace words, phrases or full sentences),

(v) using other, perhaps better, connective words or fillers,

(vi) using other words or expressions that you think are better for the information and ideas given about this contemporary issue.

<u>Exercise 5</u> Write (in around 130-150 words) a similar article, perhaps by first drawing a mind-map, and using, if you wish, similar ideas and detail to those in the suggested piece above, either:

(a) from your own experience, using your own discussion, ideas and opinions or

(b) by responding to this photo, to imagine how each of the members of this family is 'thinking' and 'feeling'.

❖ After writing your articles, have them corrected by your teacher. Then rewrite them with the corrections and improvements, and keep them in your writing file.

رسمية-6 كيف تقيّم نفسك بخصوص ما يلي: "التّسلية والصّحّة في حياتنا اليومية بين الحَيَوِيَّة والخُمول أو الكسل"؟

في 130-150 كلمة، وضّح ذلك

(أ) من خلال حياتك

(ب) من خلال حياة آخرين

(ت) مع تبيان الطرق التي يمكن أن تجعل الناس ينجذبون أكثر للطريق الصحيح كما تعتقد.

FR-6 'Leisure and health in our everyday life are shaped in the space between liveliness and apathy or laziness'? In 130-150 words (a) explain this, (b) incorporating other peoples' attitudes, and (c) how you might make them more attracted to the correct way as you see it.

أفضل شيء أن يكون تَصَرُّف (behaviour) الإنسان حسب رغبته (his desire) ولكن دون أن يؤذي نفسه أو الآخرين. إذا اختار ممارسة الرياضة أو الأعمال البدنية بعيداً عن الجلوس أمام التلفزيون طول النهار من أجل المحافظة على صحته فلا بأس (no problem). ولكن العكس لا أراه جيداً، لأنه من الصعب أن لا يؤدي الخمول إلى بعض الضرر البدني أو النفسي أو كليهما. الأفضل أن تجمع بين الفائدة والتسلية حتى لا تكون أمراً ثقيلاً على النّفس.

عندما يجمع نَمَط الحياة (way of life) بين الفائدة والمتعة (pleasure) فإنه يعطينا أوقاتاً سعيدة أثناءه (during it) وبعده. وهذا عادةً ما أحاول فعله عند اختيار (choosing) نشاط معيّن يمكن أن يتحوّل إلى هِواية (hobby) أو حتى عادة (habit).

قرّرت أن أجرّب التّنس فلم أحبه، ثم جرّبت ركض المسافات الطويلة فأعجبني كثيراً الهواء الطّلْق والحدائق والقوة التي أشعر بها. بدأ صديقي يركض معي، وإن كان يفضّل أن يتمشّى أكثر وأنا أشجّعه على طرد الكسل، فيجيب: "أنظر إلى رائد وكريم، إذا أرادا التحرّك فلا شيء باستثناء (except) الشّطرَنج (chess)! وإذا استطعت سَحبَهم (pulling them) إلى الخارج فسوف يتسكّعون (hang around) في شارع أو سوق!

مع هؤلاء ربما من المناسب دعوتهم أولاً إلى نشاطات فيها شيء من التّسكُّع كلعبة البُولِنك أو السِّهام (darts)! بعدها يمكن تشجيعهم على تسلية أكثر نشاطاً. أو يمكن الجمع بين التسلية الخاملة التي اختاروها مع شيء من

النشاط: لعبة شطرنج، وهي مفيدة لتنشيط الدماغ إذا أحببتها، ونصف ساعة من السباحة مثلاً. أو على الأقل

أن نستخدم الساقين بدلاً من وسائط النقل فنحقّق ثلاثة أهداف: النشاط وحماية البيئة وحماية الجيب!

(224 كلمة)

<u>Exercise 1</u> Study the piece above and check how successful it was in satisfying the requirements of the task by determining which paragraphs or sentences relate to which part of the task. Use colour highlighting or another form of marking for quick future reference.

<u>Exercise 2</u> Translate the underlined sentence: يمكن تشجيعهم على تسلية أكثر نشاطاً .

<u>Exercise 3</u> Explain the grammar of the two sentences in bold:

أن يؤذي نفسه أو الآخرين ، جرّبت ركض المسافات الطويلة .

<u>Exercise 4</u> How can the piece above be improved? Look into ways to make it more balanced:

(vii) in terms of how much is written for each part of the task (you may omit, add or replace words, phrases or full sentences),

(viii) using other, perhaps better, connective words or fillers,

(ix) using other words or expressions that you think are better for the ideas and description given about this never-to-be-overlooked issue.

<u>Exercise 5</u> Try to condense this piece, to reduce it to around 130-150 words, while preserving the main points.

<u>Exercise 6</u> Write (in around 130-150 words) a similar article, perhaps by first drawing a mind-map, and using, if you wish, similar ideas and detail to those in the suggested piece above, either:

(a) from your own experience, using your own discussion, ideas, opinions and suggestions

or

(b) by responding to this set of photos, which, although they show what these people are doing, might not be that clear in showing how they feel about what they are doing and why they are doing it.

❖ After writing your articles, have them corrected by your teacher. Then rewrite them with the corrections and improvements, and keep them in your writing file.

رسمية-7 أكتبي، 130-150 كلمة، مقالة

(أ) توضح، ربما من خلال تجربتك الشخصية، لماذا لا يندمج الكثير من الشباب مع احتفالات العيد في بريطانيا

(ب) إذا كنت تعتقدين أن مثل هذه المناسبات تذهب سُدىً إقترحي طرقاً لجعلها أكثر جاذبية لهم

بعكسه (ت) وضّحي لماذا لا تعتقدين أن هذه الاحتفالات مهمة.

FR-7 Write an essay (a) explaining, perhaps through your own experience, why many young people do not really engage in the *Eid* celebrations in Britain, and (b) if you believe such occasions are wasted, suggest ways to make them more appealing. Otherwise (c) explain why you do not believe these celebrations are important. (130-150 words)

لا تشعر بالعيد في بريطانيا لأنه لا توجد أماكن للشباب للقاء والتسلية. في أول يوم من العيد الفائت (previous) صلّينا صلاة العيد في المسجد، وعندما خرجنا كان الثلج قد بدأ يغطي الشوارع. ذهبنا إلى السوق لشراء هدية لأخي الصغير، ثم زرنا بيت خالتي لتهنئتهم (to express our greetings to them)، ولكننا لم نبق إلا ساعة، فقد أوصلتني أمي إلى بيت صديقتي التي هنّأتها وأهلها وأعطيتها هديتها.

في اليوم الثاني ذهبنا إلى بيت أصدقائنا ولعبنا على الكومبيوتر. وفي المساء زرنا صديقاً آخر – زيارة مملّة جداً (very boring) لأني لا أحب ابنتهم كثيرًا! البيوت تتشابه في تقديم الشاي والحلويات والمعجّنات (pastries) كالكنافة والمعمول والفطائِر.

في هذين اليومين شعرنا ببعض التغيير، ولكن المشكلة هي عدم وجود تسلية تجعلنا نشعر بالفرح الحقيقي. البعض يقول أن المشكلة هي أننا نحتفل في العيد مع الكبار الذين يفكرون بشكل مختلف، وأكثر حديثهم عن بلدانهم الأصلية ومشاكلها وهو لا يهمّنا كثيراً. وعليه، يجب أن يكون الجزء الأكبر من الاحتفال للشباب فيما بينهم، والباقي مع العائلة والأقرباء الكبار الذين نحبهم بكل تأكيد، بعكسه (otherwise) لن نجد العيد عيداً.

ربما كان اليوم الثالث أفضل، فقد ذهبنا إلى احتفال للجالية (community) في إحدى المدارس. كانت القاعة مُزيّنة، وكل عائلة جلبت بعض الحلويات. الفعاليات متنوعة كالمسابقات وتوزيع الهدايا. مثل هذا سيكون على الأكثر أفضل من زيارات البيوت.

أستطيع القول أن العيد هذه السنة كان أفضل، وإن كان بارداً بالقِياس (in comparison) إلى العيد في البلدان العربية كما حضرتها شخصياً في إحدى السفرات. (218 كلمة)

Exercise 1 Study the piece above and check how successful it was in satisfying the requirements of the task by determining which paragraphs or sentences relate to which part of the task. Use colour highlighting or another form of marking for quick future reference.

Exercise 2 Translate the underlined words: زرنا ، نحتفل ، جلبت .

Exercise 3 Give the grammar of each of the following words in the following, after

separating it into its constituents: هنأتها وأهلها وأعطيتها هديتها .

Exercise 4 How can the piece above be improved? Look into ways to make it more balanced:

(x)   in terms of how much is written for each part of the task (you may omit, add or replace words, phrases or full sentences),

(xi)   using other, perhaps better, connective words or fillers,

(xii) using other words or expressions that you think are better for the description given about this kind of social celebration.

Exercise 5 Write (in around 130-150 words) a similar article, perhaps by first drawing a mind-map, and using, if you wish, similar ideas and detail to those in the suggested piece above, either:

(a) from your own experience, using your own discussion, ideas, opinions and suggestions

or

(b) by responding to these two photos showing people celebrating Eid, one in the UK and the other in the Middle East.

❖ After writing your articles, have them corrected by your teacher. Then rewrite them with the corrections and improvements, and keep them in your writing file.

رسمية-8 أكتب 130-150 كلمة حول الآتي:

(أ) هل القراءة جزء مهم من حياتنا؟ (ب) كيف تتعاملين أنت مع القراءة؟

(ت) كيف أن ما تقومين به يختلف عن آخرين؟

FR-8 Write 130-150 words on the following: (a) Is reading important in our life? (b) What is your attitude towards reading? (c) How is your way different to that of others?

If you like, you can use some of the following paragraphs and sentences as starters or to give you ideas for writing this article.

الكثير من الناس مُولَعون (fond of) بقراءة القصص، ولا سيما ...

غيرهم يقرأون أي شيء، القراءة عبارة عن ...

ولكنني أتساءل: هل أقرأ شيئاً لا ينفع عملياً؟ البعض يقول: بَلى، لأن ...

على أية حال، مزاجي (my taste) يختلف قليلاً، فإني ...

أتمنى أن أقرأ موضوعات كثيرة، ولكن الوقت محدود، لهذا ...

أنا وصديقتي زينب نعتبر القراءة من ضروريات الحياة، حيث ...

كما ونحب أن ننقل ما قرأنا، لأن تَعميم (spreading) الفائدة يجعلنا نشعر بقيمة ...

As you can see, you don't need to attend to the points of the task according to their sequence in the question; you can mix them as you go along with the piece. But make sure that all points are included.

Try to use interesting 'connective words' such as the words with wavy underlines used above to link the sentences in a way that flows, and at the same time to start the other part of your description or explanation.

Don't overlook your punctuation and handwriting.

<u>Exercise1</u> Translate the words with <u>wavy underlines</u>.

<u>Exercise 2</u> A blogger wrote: 'Whatever you say, reading from the net can never beat reading from a paper book!' Do you agree with her position, and why? Also, do you find that writing this on her blog page on the internet is somewhat contradictory, for her blog might have indeed 'beaten' the paper book?! Write 130-150 words.

❖ After writing your articles, have them corrected by your teacher. Then rewrite them with the corrections and improvements, and keep them in your writing file.

رسمية-9 أكتب عن الموسيقى

(أ) كيف هي بالنسبة إليك

(ب) أنواع الآلات أو الموسيقى

ربما (ت) من خلال حفلة موسيقية حضرتها أو شاهدتها من التلفاز أو الانترنت، تذكر فيها المكان والحضور

والعازفين والموسيقى وأية تفاصيل أخرى.

أكتب 130-150 كلمة.

FR-9 Write about music: (a) how do you feel about music, (b) types of music and instruments, perhaps (c) through a music event that you went to or watched on TV or on the internet, mentioning the place, audience, players, music and any other details? Write 130-150 words.

بيانو (piano) بوق (trumpet) عود (oud) كمان (violin) غير ذلك لا يهمني، المهم ما يخرج من ألحان تُلامس (touches) القلب بعد أن تدخل الأُذُن. بالنسبة لي الموسيقى كاللوحات السريالية (sureal) التي لا أفهم منها شيئاً ولكنها جميلة أقف أمامها طويلاً مستمتعاً بالتّكوين (composition) والألوان.

صديق صديقي فائز يعزِف (plays) الجيتار في فرقة (band) من أربعة شباب، دعاني فائز إلى حفل موسيقي (concert) محلي تشارك فيه الفرقة. تصورت أنني سأجلس في مسرح لا أكاد أتنفس كما هو الحال في حفلات الأوركسترا الوطنية ومقطوعاتها الكلاسيكية (classic) التي تتطلب صمتاً تاماً من الجمهور الذي يُصغي (listen) تماماً، إلا أنني – ولأن فائز لم يخبرني – وجدت نفسي في حديقة عامة تنتشر فيها ست فرق، في كل منها ثلاثة أو أربعة أو خمسة يعزفون مختلف الآلات الموسيقية، بعضها جمع الشرقي مع الغربي في مزيج جميل عموماً، وأحياناً غير مُنسَجِم (in disharmony).

طبعاً لا يعزف الجميع في آنٍ واحد – يتناوبون بطريقة جديدة: كل فرقة تعزف خمس دقائق فقط، ثم الفرقة على الجانب الآخر المقابل، ثم ثالثة وهكذا، وفي أثناء العزف تقوم الفرق الأخرى ببيع تسجيلاتها على أقراص (CDs) لها أو بطاقات دعاية (promotion) فيها استعدادها لإحياء حفلات عيد الميلاد والزواج وغيرها.

كان مهرجاناً صغيراً، تجلس حيث تريد وتتحدث مع العازفين وأنت تسمع الموسيقى التي تعزفها الفرق الواحدة تِلو الأخرى (one after the other) بقربك أو بعيداً عنك. كان يوماً جميلاً حقاً.   (194 كلمة)

Exercise 1 Study the piece above and check how successful it was in satisfying the requirements of the task by determining which paragraphs or sentences relate to which part of the task. Use colour highlighting or another form of marking for quick future reference.

Exercise 2

(a) What is the grammar of the words in bold? بعيداً ، أحياناً ، عموماً

(b) What is the grammar of the sentence in bold? كان يوماً جميلاً حقاً

Exercise 3 Translate the following <u>underlined words</u>: مستمتعاً ، صمتاً ، يعزف ، يتناوبون .

Exercise 4 How can the piece above be improved? Look into ways to make it more balanced:

(xiii) in terms of how much is written for each part of the task (you may omit, add or replace words, phrases or full sentences),

(xiv) using other, perhaps better, connective words or fillers,

(xv) using other words or expressions that you think are better for the description given about that music event.

Exercise 5 Write (in around 130-150 words) a similar article, perhaps by first drawing a mind-map, and using, if you wish, similar ideas and detail to those in the suggested piece above, or better still, try to write about your own experience and, most important, your own opinion and views on music, either:

(a) from your own experience

or

(b) by responding to this photo, to imagine how enjoyable or not such a music event might be and whether or not you expect that you would enjoy the performance.

❖ After writing your articles, have them corrected by your teacher. Then rewrite them with the corrections and improvements, and keep them in your writing file.

رسمية-10 لماذا نرى دائماً أشخاصاً يلعبون أو يمارسون كرة القدم أو كرة السلة أو الكرة الطائرة وما شابه من أنواع الرياضة ولكن لا نكاد نعرف أحداً يمارس المُصارعة أو رَفع الأثقال؟

أكتب، في 130-150 كلمة

(أ) تفسيرك (ب) نظرتك حول هذه الأنواع المختلفة من الرياضة.

FR-10 Why do we see people playing or practising football, basketball, volleyball and similar sports, but we hardly know anyone who engages in wrestling or weightlifting? Write, in 130-150 words, your explanation, along with your views about these different types of sports.

هذان نوعان مختلفان تماماً من النشاطات الرياضية، وذلك في الجهد المبذول (spent)، والتدريب (training) المطلوب، والعلاقة مع الرياضي الآخر، والمرافق المتوفرة.

من يفضّل ألعاب الكرة الجماعية (team) فإنه لا يحتاج إلى تدريب شديد، خصوصاً إذا كانت للتسلية فقط. وحتى إذا كان عُضواً (member) في فَريق فإن زملاءه اللاعبين يُعَوِّضون (make up) عنه إذا لم يلعب جيداً. أما المصارعة فإن من يُقَرِّر (decides) ممارستها يحتاج إلى مدرِّب (coach) يعلمه كيف يتدرّب (train) على الحركات الهجومية والدفاعية وكيفية التّخلُّص من محاولات المصارع الخصم (opponent)، إضافة إلى نادٍ (club) فيه دورات المصارعة وهذه غير متوفرة كثيراً. ثم عليه أن يعلم أنها رياضة شديدة فيها الجهد والقوّة، وأحياناً بعض العَداء (enmity) مع الخَصم، وربما بعض الرّضوض (bruises) والكسور!

وأما رفع الأثقال فهي تشابه المصارعة في ما تحتاجه من تدريب وجهد ونادٍ، ولكن دون مشاكل مع الرّبّاعين (weightlifters) الآخرين. أيضاً، فيها جانب أجده جذّاباً وهو أنها تضع أهدافاً واضحة للرياضي، وهي الأرقام (records) التي يريد تحطيمها (breaking them)، وكل مرة يصل إلى رقم جديد يعطيه ذلك دَفعة (push) كبيرة جداً فيستمر في التمرين مجدّداً أكثر.

أخيراً، حتى إذا كنت تحب الرياضة الفردية فيمكن أن تجد في السّباحة أو الجَري (running) ما تريد، وهما رياضتان أكيد تحتاجان إلى تمرين (training) وجهد ولكن ليس كالمصارعة أو رفع الأثقال. كما أن المسابح متوفرة للأولى، والشوارع والحدائق والدنيا كلها متوفرة لمن يريد أن يجري (runs) ليلاً ونهاراً! (194 كلمة)

Exercise 1 Study the piece above and check how successful it was in satisfying the requirements of the task by determining which paragraphs or sentences relate to which part of the task. Use colour highlighting or another form of marking for quick future reference (different underlining styles are used to highlight connective words, fillers and useful words).

<u>Exercise 2</u> Translate the following: underlined words: وذلك ، وخصوصاً ، إضافة إلى ، كما .

<u>Exercise 3</u> What grammatical position does each of the words in bold have (two related topics are involved)? مختلفان ، الرياضية ، جذاباً ، جداً

<u>Exercise 4</u> How can the piece above be improved? Look into ways to make it more balanced:
 (xvi) in terms of how much is written for each part of the task (you may omit, add or replace words, phrases or full sentences),
 (xvii) using other, perhaps better, connective words or fillers,
 (xviii) using other words or expressions that you think are better for the information and ideas given about this issue and the comparison included in it.

<u>Exercise 5</u> Write (in around 130-150 words) a similar article, perhaps by first drawing a mind-map, and using, if you wish, similar ideas and detail to those in the suggested piece above, either:
(a) from your own experience, using your own discussion, ideas and opinions
or
(b) by responding to these two photos, describing what do you see in the athletes - mind, body and spirit.

❖ After writing your articles, have them corrected by your teacher. Then rewrite them with the corrections and improvements, and keep them in your writing file.

LOCAL AREA, HOLIDAY AND TRAVEL

رسمية-11 الكثير من المهاجرين يحاولون أخذ أولادهم، الذين وُلدوا ونشؤوا في بريطانيا، إلى بلدانهم الأصلية، ظانين أن أولادهم مثلهم متحمسون لذلك، مع أن الكثير منهم ليسوا كذلك أو لديهم مشاعر مختلطة حوله. ناقش هذا، في 130-150 كلمة، ربما اعتماداً على تجربتك الشخصية أو تجربة شخص تعرفه، ذاكراً أي نقاط إيجابية أوسلبية يمكن أن تتضمنها مثل هذه السفرات.

FR-11 Most immigrant parents try to take their children, born and raised in the UK, to their countries of origin, thinking that their children are as keen as they are to do so; however many are not, or have mixed feelings towards it. Discuss this, in 130-150 words, perhaps using your own experience or that of someone you know, mentioning any good and bad points such trips may have.

في عطلة عيد الفِصْح (Easter) ذهبت إلى العراق. كنت أحب لقاء الأقرباء وأنتظر كثيراً أن أرى آثار حضارة وادي النَّهرَين (the civilization of Mesopotamia) التي قرأت عنها.

أقلَعَت الطائرة (the plane departed) من لندن ولما هَبطت (arrived) في المطار كانت الحرارة أعلى بعشرين درجة! إستقبلني الأقارب بفرح شديد، وكانوا يتنازعون (they quarrel, i.e. compete) على القيام بواجب الضِيافة (hospitality)، فقد كُنتُ أتغدّى (I have lunch) في بيت وأتعشّى (I have supper) في آخر! هذا الاهتمام عَوّض (compensated for) الإحساس بقلّة الأهل في بريطانيا.

كي نزور الأقارب في بغداد كنا نتنقل بين الأعظمية والصليخ والكاظمية والمنصور والمسبح، ولكل منها شكل مُميّز (distinguished). أعجبني شارع أبي نُؤاس الواقع على نهر دجلة، وخرجنا في جولة في النهر مساءً (evening). ذهبنا إلى المتحف العراقي المليء بآثار العراق القديمة، والمتحف البغدادي أيضاً. أحببت اختلاف المكان، لكنّي بقيت أُقارن (compare) بين التنظيم والنظافة هناك وفي لندن.

زرنا آثار بابِل (Babylon) القديمة، وبعدها توجّهنا إلى كربلاء لزيارة مرقَد (tomb) الحسين بن علي، ثم توجّهنا لزيارة مرقد الإمام علي بن أبي طالب في النجف وبيته في الكوفة القريبة. شعرت بفرح وأنا أتنقل في مناطق تاريخية مهمة، متحمسة كيف سأحكي لأصدقائي عن هذا عند عودتي.

بعد أيام، زرنا سامرّاء، وقبل أن نصلها بمسافة لاحَتْ (appeared) المَلُويّة الشهيرة وهي مِئذَنة حَلَزُونيّة (spiral minaret)، ثم بدأت القُبّة الذهبية (golden dome) للإمامين العسكريّين تظهر إلى جهة اليمين.

في اليوم الثاني، قضينا **ساعات** في مزرعة جدّي، وكنا نتناول أنواع الفاكهة من الأشجار مباشرة، ولا يعرف أحد كم أكلنا في ذلك اليوم! هذه تجربة أخرى جديدة لي، جمعت بين التسلية والفرح باهتمام العشيرة (tribe) وبالفخر بأصول والداي إلى بلد عريق (deep-rooted) ومهم وجميل.

هذه الأمور: التاريخ الحاضر إلى اليوم، والدين، مع التسلية والتغيير، موجودة، بدرجات مختلفة، في البلاد العربية، وأعتقد أن أكثرية الشباب سيشكرون أهلهم إذا أخذوهم إلى زيارة بلدانهم الأصلية.   (251 كلمة)

Exercise 1 Study the piece above and check how successful it was in satisfying the requirements of the task by determining which paragraphs or sentences relate to which part of the task. Use colour highlighting or another form of marking for quick future reference.

Exercise 2 Translate the <u>underlined sentence</u>:

وأعتقد أن أكثرية الشباب سيشكرون أهلهم إذا أخذوهم إلى زيارة بلدانهم الأصلية

Exercise 3 What grammatical position does each of the words in bold have?

الأقرباء ، الأقارب ، الأقارب ، هناك ، عند

Exercise 4 How can the piece above be improved? Look into ways to make it more balanced:

(xix) in terms of how much is written for each part of the task (you may omit, add or replace words, phrases or full sentences),

(xx) using other, perhaps better, connective words or fillers,

(xxi) using other words or expressions that you think are better for the information and description given about this holiday trip to the parents' country of origin.

Exercise 5 Try to condense this piece, to reduce it to around 130-150 words, while preserving the main points.

Exercise 6 Write (in around 130-150 words) a similar article, perhaps by first drawing a mind-map, and using, if you wish, similar ideas and detail to those in the suggested piece above, either:

(a) from your own experience, using your own discussion, ideas, opinions and suggestions

or

(b) by trying to figure out/imagine the love, expectations, differences and all the other things that span the gaps between three generations, the third of whom are living in the UK, that you see sitting in a coffee shop.

❖ After writing your articles, have them corrected by your teacher. Then rewrite them with the corrections and improvements, and keep them in your writing file.

رسمية-12 أكتبي 130-150 كلمة حول عطلة مع عائلتك، فيها: (أ) سبب تنظيم عائلتك للسفرة (ب) رأيك

في قضاء سفرة العطلة مع العائلة (ت) مشكلة حصلت عند وصولكم (ث) "عطلة الأحلام" بالنسبة إليك.

FR-12 Write 130-150 words on a holiday trip with your family, addressing the following points: (a) why your family arranged the trip, (b) your view of spending the holiday with your family, (c) a problem that occurred on your arrival, (d) what your 'dream' holiday would be.

If you like, you can use some of the following paragraphs and sentences as starters or to give you ideas for writing this article.

لأن أبي لا يرانا كثيراً أثناء الدوام، فقد قرر ...

تحمّست أمي هي الأخرى، لأن ...

كنت قلقة (worried) أن نعيش نفس جو البيت في السفرة، ...

ولكن النتيجة كانت مقبولة، حيث أن ...

وحسب المثل الشائع "رُبَّ ضارّةٍ نافعة" (a blessing in disguise)، فبمُجَرَّد أنْ/ ما أنْ (as soon as) وصلنا ...

فعلى الرّغم (although) من أننا أضعنا يومين في هذه المشكلة، إلا أن ...

أفضل عطلة في نظري هي ...

وذلك لأنني أتصور ...

In the above starters, the points of the task are attended to according to their sequence in the question. Although this is a reasonable, straightforward approach, you can write about the points of the task in any order. But make sure that all points are included.

In addition, you can see that there are two starting statements for every point of the task. This again is a reasonable way to make your piece balanced. That said, some points might need to be assigned a longer portion of the piece, in which case you could write more or longer paragraphs for them.

Try to use interesting openers so as to tick your 'variety' box when the examiner corrects your paper. Bear in mind that variety is not confined to starting ideas, but can be applied to the piece as a whole - in vocabulary, grammar and the manner of your expression.

❖ **After writing your article, have it corrected by your teacher. Then rewrite it with the corrections and improvements, and keep it in your writing file.**

<u>Exercise</u> Translate each of the words in bold after separating it into its constituents:

أضعنا ، وصلنا ، يرانا.

رسمية-**13** أكتب، في **150-130** كلمة، ما ينبغي عمله بخصوص ترتيبات السفر والسكن من أجل تفادي أية خسائر أو خيبة أمل؛ ربما تستطيع الاستفادة من تجربة حقيقية عندك.

FR-13 Describe, in 130-150 words, what one should do when making travel arrangements to avoid any mishaps or disappointments; perhaps you could use a real-life experience as an example.

Let's start here by drawing a mind-map containing the ideas, giving some details.

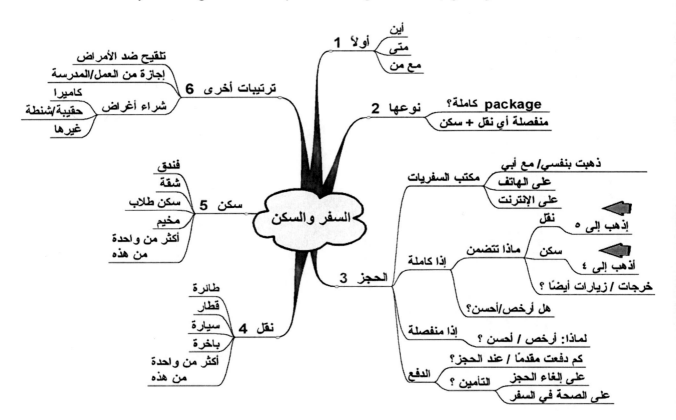

This mind-map contains alternatives. Your mind-map should be smaller and more customized. It could look like the one on the next page.

Use this mind-map to write the article. Alternatively, you can draw your own mind-map, based on the first one. Decide first the branches which are relevant. Then decide the number of words for each branch.

You might consider adding other alternatives, such as: ticket, one-way ticket, return ticket, discounts, ferry, youth hostel, villa, internet booking, obtaining a visa, or any relevant words from the following (incomplete) vocabulary.

قاعَة سكن dormitory	room with bathroom غرفة مع حَمّام	hotel فُندُق/ أُوتيل
مَوقع كَرَفان caravan site	bed and breakfast سرير وفُطُور/ إفطار	flat/apartment شُقَّة
مُخَيَّم camp	house/villa/chalet بيت/ فيلاّ/ شاليه	youth hostel بُيوت الشَّباب

تَدْفِئَة heating	تَخْفيض reduction	إقامَة كامِلَة (تَشْمُل جَميع الوَجَبات)
تكييف هَواء air conditioning	مُقَدَّماً in advance	full board (all meals included)
بَياضات الأسِرَّة bed linen	تَرْفيه entertainment	غُرْفَة مُفْرَدَة single room
		twin-bedded room غرفة بِسَريرَيْن

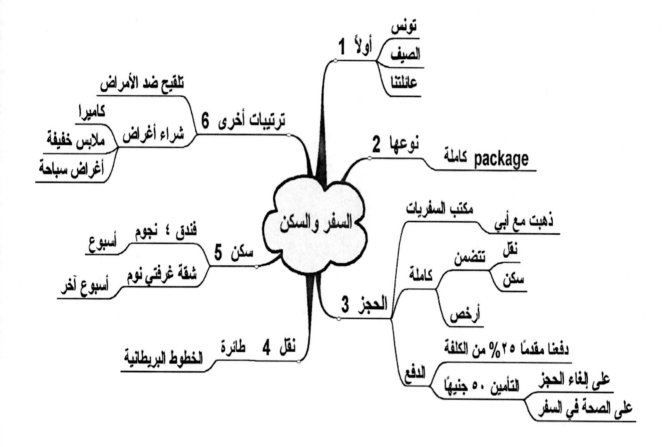

You should try to avoid writing the above details as they are, in bullet points or similar. Instead, write them in paragraphs of balanced sizes, with good structure benefiting from varied grammatical forms and the use of connecting words.

Pay attention also to your punctuation and handwriting.

<u>Exercise 1</u> Translate the following words (in the second mind-map): حجز ، تلقيح ، التأمين .

<u>Exercise 2</u> Explain the grammar of the two sentences (in the mind-maps):

لماذا أرخص؟ ، ذهبت مع أبي.

❖ After writing your article, have it corrected by your teacher. Then rewrite it with the corrections and improvements, and keep it in your writing file.

رسمية-14 "لن تصدقوا ما حصل لنا في سفرتنا الماضية!" أكتب 130-150 كلمة تقصّ فيها الذي حصل

معك، أو مع فرد/ أفراد من عائلتك، أو مع أشخاص تعرفهم – حادثة أو مشكلة أو ما شابه، تتضمن الآتي:

(أ) أين حصلت (ب) ما الذي حصل (ت) ماذا فعلتم/ فعلوا (ث) كيف تأثرت السفرة – سلبياً أو إيجابياً.

FR-14 'You will never believe what happened to us on our last trip.' Write 130-150 words about what happened to you, or to member(s) of your family or people you know, addressing the following:

(a) when it happened, (b) what happened, (c) what did you or they do, (d) how was the trip affected, in a good or bad way or both, by this.

If you like, you can use some of the following paragraphs and sentences as starters or to give you ideas for writing this article.

كلا، لم يسرقنا أحد أول ما وصلنا! ولم ... ولم ...

ما حصل في سفرتنا "السفاري" إلى كينيا غريب ومضحك حقاً.

كانت السفرة إلى محمية طبيعية (national reserve)، وهي ...

وكان علاء قد صدّع رؤوسنا عنها لعدة أشهر... وأن الأمان ...

أما ما حصل فكان شيئاً آخر! فقد ...

بقينا أكثر من أربع ساعات في ... ونحن ننتظر ...

بعد انتهاء المِحنة (ordeal) كانت أختي وأمي في حالة ... وقد قررتا أن ...

فشلنا أنا وأبي في إقناعهما ... ولهذا تقلّصت مدة ...

إلا أن ما حصل، والصور التي أخذناها، والتي ظهرت في ...

هكذا تكون السفرة وإلاّ فلا (otherwise no point)!

In the above starters, the points of the task are attended to according to their sequence in the question, especially in such a task that contains a story and consequences.

In this task, some points might need to be assigned a longer portion of the piece, in which case you could write more or longer paragraphs for them.

Try to use interesting openers (rather than the obvious ones) so as to tick your 'variety' box when the examiner corrects your paper. Bear in mind that variety is not confined to starting ideas, but can be applied to the piece as a whole - in vocabulary, grammar and the manner of your expression.

Don't overlook your punctuation and handwriting.

❖ After writing your article, have it corrected by your teacher. Then rewrite it with the corrections and improvements, and keep it in your writing file.

رسمية-15 "لن أترك كتابي المفضل من أجل حفلة لا معنى لها!" "السير تحت المطر من أجل مشاهدة عرض مسرحي مفيد أكثر بكثير من الجلوس في دفء غرفة المعيشة لمشاهدة مباراة كرة قدم بائسة!"

(أ) هل توافقين على أن الرياضة والحفلات تأخذ أكثر مما ينبغي من وقت الشباب، بالتأكيد أكثر من أنواع أخرى من التسلية كالقراءة والمسرح والرسم والتصوير؟

(ب) هل توافقين أنه ينبغي للشباب أن يجربوا مختلف أنواع النشاطات المسلية؟

في 130-150 كلمة وضحي أجوبتك سواء كانت بالموافقة أو العكس.

FR-15 'I will not give up reading my favourite book for a pointless party!' 'Walking in the rain to watch a play in a theatre is much more rewarding than sitting in the warmth of my living room to watch a stupid match of football!'
(a) Do you agree that sports or parties take up too much of young peoples' time, and certainly more than other types of entertainment such as reading, theatre, drawing, photography?
(b) Do you agree that young people should try different types of leisure activities? In 130-150 words explain your answers either way.

من المؤكّد أنّ الرياضة تأخذ وقتاً أكثر من أنواع التسلية الأخرى، وأن مشاهدتها على التلفاز أكثر من ممارستها، والسبب هو برامج الرياضة الكثيرة والنقل المباشر (live coverage) للمباريات والبطولات التي تستمر أسابيع كدورة ومبلِدن وبطولة أوروبا. ولكن الشباب يحبون الرياضة، حتى ولو كانت ضمن الحياة اليومية كالمشي والركض والدراجات، وهي مفيدة لهم.

أما الحفلات فليست كثيرة لأنها في مناسبات محدّدة ولا تأخذ وقتاً، كأعياد الميلاد، حتى ولا حفلات الكبار التي ندعى إليها كحفلات الأعراس.

شخصياً، دائماً عندي ما أقرؤه ، سواء من الأعمال الأدبية (literary) كالقِصّة (story) أو الرّواية (novel) أو دِيوان لأحد الشُّعَراء (poets)، أو الكتب العلمية أو الدينية أو عادات الشّعوب التي أهتَمّ بها (I am interested in) وأحب مُعرفتها. وبين الحينِ والآخر (every now and then) أذهب لِمُشاهدة مسرحيّة، أحياناً أقرأ عنها أولاً، أو نكون قد درسناها في المدرسة.

الشباب لا يفعلون هذا إلا البعض منهم، لأن المِزاج (taste) يختلف، فلا يجوز أن نُجبِر (we force) أحداً على قراءة قصة إذا كان لا يحب ذلك. ممكن أنه يحب مُشاهدة الفيلم بدلاً من قراءة القصّة. أستطيع الجلوس مع أبي ساعات نستمع إلى الموسيقى الكلاسيكية فإذا ما رأتنا أختي خرجت وهي تضحك عالياً!

أما الفنون التّشكيليّة (fine arts) كالرّسم والتّصوير الفوتوغرافي فهذه عالم آخر، لأنها تحتاج إلى الرّغبة وربما موهبة (talent)، ولكن يمكن ممارستها دون موهبة لأن المهم هو قضاء وقت طيّب.

أخيراً، أتصور أن تجربة أنواع مختلفة من التسلية والنشاطات صحيح لمعرفة ما إذا كانت هذه التسلية تناسبني أو تعجبني أو أستطيع القيام بها. وحتى إذا لم تعجبني فإني لم أخسر شيئاً.   (224 كلمة)

<u>Exercise 1</u> Study the piece above and check how successful it was in satisfying the requirements of the task. Use colour highlighting or another form of marking for quick future reference.

<u>Exercise 2</u> Give the full grammar of the sentence in bold: الشباب لا يفعلون هذا إلا **البعض منهم** .

<u>Exercise 3</u> How can the piece above be improved? Look into ways to make it more balanced:

(xxii) in terms of how much is written for each part of the task (you may omit, add or replace words, phrases or full sentences),

(xxiii) using other, perhaps better, connective words or fillers,

(xxiv) using other words or expressions that you think are better for the opinions and ideas given about this issue.

<u>Exercise 4</u> Try to condense this piece, to reduce it to around 130-150 words, while preserving the main points.

<u>Exercise 5</u> Write (in around 130-150 words) a similar article, perhaps by first drawing a mind-map, and using, if you wish, similar ideas and detail to those in the suggested piece above, either:

(a) from your own experience, using your own discussion, ideas, opinions and suggestions

or

(b) by responding to this advertisement announcing the imminent arrival of a famous band, which encourages the purchase of tickets without delay, and describing the reaction that you might expect from some young men and women compared to the reaction of others.

لأول مرة على مسرح المدينة
أمسية موسيقية غنائية فريدة
مع الفرقة الشبابية الصاعدة
شرق.West
إحجزوا تذاكركم قبل نفادها
من شباك التذاكر في المسرح
10 صباحاً – 3 عصراً

❖ After writing your articles, have them corrected by your teacher. Then rewrite them with the corrections and improvements, and keep them in your writing file.

رسمية-16 إذا أُعطيت الفرصة لإدخال تحسينات على منطقتك، خصوصاً أماكن التسلية،

(أ) ماذا ستفعل، و (ب) لماذا؟

(ت) هل شاركت أو يشارك الشباب واليافعون في مثل هذا؟

أكتب 130-150 كلمة.

FR-16 If you were given the opportunity to introduce improvements to your area, especially places of entertainment, what would you do, and why? And have you participated - or do young people participate - in such projects? Write 130-150 words.

في منطقتنا الكثير/ العديد/ القليل (a lot/many/few) من أماكن التسلية. ففي الشارع الرئيسي دار سينما تعرض الأفلام الحديثة التي أحبها. وعلى مَقرُبة منها (nearby it) مطعمان ومقهى؛ كما توجد متاجر صغيرة، أحدها يبيع الأفلام والألعاب الإلكترونية. ثم هناك نادٍ للألعاب الإلكترونية بالليزر وغيره صار مَقصداً (popular) destination)) للشباب. إلا أن الحصول على مكان للسيارة صعب جداً، فهذه الشوارع بحاجة إلى موقف سيارات (car park) بطابقين أو أكثر.

طبعاً هذا يجب أن تقوم به البلدية. ولكننا نستطيع المساعدة في تحسينات أخرى، كما فعلنا في المشاركة في حملة (campaign) صبغ للجدران والأعمدة وغيرها خارج محطة القطار.

في الجهة الأخرى يوجد المركز الترفيهي، وفيه مسبح وملعب مغلق (indoor)، لكنه لا يَفِي بالغَرَض (is not enough) لأن عدد الناس كبير ودائماً ننتظر طويلاً. لذا، من الضروري بناء ملعب آخر، وحمّامات إضافية.

مثل هذا المكان يجب أن يهتم بتوفير غرفة ألعاب للصغار يتعلمون التركيب والتجميع والألوان. عندنا غرفة صغيرة في المركز، تقوم أختي وصديقاتها بمساعدة الأمهات في نهاية الأسبوع، ويشعرن بسعادة مع الأطفال.

خارج المنطقة ملعب مَهجُور (deserted)، سيكون مناسباً لِمِضمار (track) للسيارات الكهربائية وسيارات الوقود الصغيرة، وهي تسلية يحبها الشباب ولكنها غير متوفّرة.

شمال منطقتنا توجد حديقة عامة كبيرة، فيها مطعم نذهب إليه أحياناً. على إحدى جهاتها مساحة خالية، لو كان الأمر بيدي لأقَمْتُ فيها مُربّى مائي (aquarium) صغير، وسيأتي بدَخَل (income) من السّفرات المدرسية

وزيارات الناس. <u>بالمناسبة</u>. شاركت مدرستنا في مسابقة زرع شُجيرات (bushes) في الجانب الشمالي من الحديقة – فكانت تسلية ومنافسة وفائدة.

أحب القراءة، وأعتبر المكتبة العامة إحدى أهم وسائل الترفيه. والحمد لله في منطقتنا مكتبتان توفران الكتب والمجلات والأقراص المدمجة، لكنهما تَفتَقِران (lack) إلى الأثاث الحديث، كما لا يوجد كتب حاسوبية. عندنا الآن مشروع يشترك فيه اليافعون، تُجمع الكتب التي يريد الناس التخلص منها، **وتضاف** إلى المكتبة العامة الصغيرة، <u>وبالفعل</u> جُمعت كتب كثيرة **وأضيفت** إلى المكتبة، وهذا يشجعنا على المزيد.   (268 كلمة)

<u>Exercise 1</u> Study the piece above and check how successful it was in satisfying the requirements of the task by determining which paragraphs or sentences relate to which part of the task. Use colour highlighting or another form of marking for quick future reference.

<u>Exercise 2</u> Translate the underlined words: إلا أن ، طبعاً ، وبالمناسبة ، وبالفعل .

<u>Exercise 3</u>

(a) Explain the grammar of the words in bold: تضاف ، أضيفت .

(b) What is the grammar topic here? <u>لو كان الأمر بيدي لأَقَمْتُ فيها مُربّى</u>

<u>Exercise 4</u> How can the piece above be improved? Look into ways to make it more balanced:
  (xxv) in terms of how much is written for each part of the task (you may omit, add or replace words, phrases or full sentences),
  (xxvi) using other, perhaps better, connective words or fillers,
  (xxvii) using other words or expressions that you think are better for the description, ideas and opinions given about this interesting and quite useful experience that many young people might be enthusiastic about.

<u>Exercise 5</u> Write (in around 130-150 words) a similar article, perhaps by first drawing a mind-map, and using, if you wish, similar ideas and detail to those in the suggested piece above, from your own experience, using your own discussion, ideas, opinions and suggestions.

❖ After writing your articles, have them corrected by your teacher. Then rewrite them with the corrections and improvements, and keep them in your writing file.

▰▰▰▰ SCHOOL ▰▰▰▰

رسمية-17 أكتب مقالة من 130-150 كلمة تحت عنوان "أنا والمدرسة"، تذكر فيها

(أ) نوع مدرستك، ومستواها بين المدارس

(ب) المواضيع التي تدرسها

(ت) هل أن مرافقها وتجهيزاتها جيدة

(ث) لو أردت تغيير شيئين فقط فما هما، ولماذا؟

FR-17 Write an essay in 130-150 words entitled 'Me and my school', mentioning in it (a) the type of school you attend, (b) the subjects you study, (c) how good or otherwise are its premises and equipment, and (d) if you wanted to change just two things, what are they and why?

مدرستي من المدارس الحكومية في منطقتنا، للمرحلتين المتوسطة/ الإعدادية (intermediate/pre-GCSE and GCSE) والثانوية (high school/A-level)، للذكور فقط (males only/all-boys). وهي **تعد** من المدارس المتوسطة حسب نتائجها في الامتحانات العامة (public exams)، يتحسن أداؤها (its performance) **تدريجياً** كل سنة.

أدرس مجموعة من المواضيع، بعضها إجباري (compulsory) لجميع الطلاب، وأهمها اللغة الانجليزية والأدب الانجليزي والرياضيات والعلوم، وبعضها اختياري (optional) وذلك في اللغات — حيث اخترت اللغة الإسبانية — وفي الإنسانيات (humanities) وقد اخترت التاريخ وفي مجالات أخرى — وقد اخترت دراسات الأعمال (business studies) والرسم. أتصور أنها مجموعة متنوعة من المواضيع ستساعدني في آخر الأمر على اختيار المواضيع التي أريد دراستها في الثانوية **تحضيراً** للجامعة.

أما بنايات المدرسة فاثنتان قديمة واثنتان أحدث، ولكن التصميم قديم خصوصاً في الداخل، يحتاج إلى تحديث (modernisation) ولكن — كما تعرفون — العُذر (excuse) دائماً هو الميزانية (budget)! على أن التجهيزات الداخلية، من رحلات وكراسي، والمختبرات أيضاً، لا سيما مختبر الفيزياء ومختبر اللغات، حديثة وملونة بألوان بهيجة (cheerful). المشكلة في صغر مساحة الألعاب والرياضة لأن آخر بناية بُنيت أكلت الكثير من الساحة.

ما أريد تغييره؟ مؤكد أكثر من شيئين! ولكن أهم شيئين هما:

الأول أن يسمح لنا بالبقاء في المدرسة ساعتين بعد انتهاء الدوام من أجل أن نقوم بكتابة الواجبات البيتية

(homework)، فهذا سيساعد الطلاب الذين لهم ظروف غير مساعدة في البيت؛

الثاني أن تُهدم (knocked down) قاعة المدرسة وتُبنى واحدة جديدة، لأنها قديمة وكئيبة، ويمكن القيام بحملة

تبرعات (donations) للمساعدة في جمع المال اللازم لهذا.　　(199 كلمة)

<u>Exercise 1</u> The piece above has attended to the points of the task in the same sequence as a question, which is quite reasonable. But study it to see how successful it was in expressing the ideas. Use colour highlighting or another form of marking for quick future reference.

<u>Exercise 2</u>

(a) Name the grammar topic that relates to the words in bold: تعد ، بنيت ، يسمح ، تهد .

(b) What is the grammar of the words in bold? تحضيراً ، تدريجياً

<u>Exercise 3</u> How can the piece above be improved? Look into ways to make it more balanced:

(xxviii)　　in terms of how much is written for each part of the task (you may omit, add or replace words, phrases or full sentences),

(xxix) using other, perhaps better, connective words or fillers,

(xxx) using other words or expressions that you think are better for the description and suggestions given about this subject, which is common to millions of students.

<u>Exercise 4</u> Write (in around 130-150 words) a similar article, perhaps by first drawing a mind-map, and using, if you wish, similar ideas and detail to those in the suggested piece above, either:

(a) from your own experience, using your own discussion, ideas, opinions and suggestions, and following a different sequence
or

(b) by responding to this photo, imagining the feelings of the students, and teachers, working in this school, and what ideas they might have that reflect their feelings.

❖ After writing your articles, have them corrected by your teacher. Then rewrite them with the corrections and improvements, and keep them in your writing file.

رسمية-18 أكتب 130-150 كلمة في وصف يومك المدرسي:

(أ) الجدول الزمني لليوم

(ب) كيف تسير مع الحصص الدراسية

(ت) الفرص وفرصة الغداء

(ث) قبل وبعد المدرسة

(ج) أية تفاصيل أخرى تجدها ذات صِلة.

FR-18 Write 130-150 words describing your typical school day, including: (a) the timetable of your day, (b) how you go about your lessons, (c) breaks and lunch hour, (d) before and after school, and (e) any other detail you think relevant.

If you like, you can use some of the following paragraphs and sentences as starters or to give you ideas for writing this article.

أذهب إلى المدرسة الساعة الثامنة والنصف ... لأن مدرستي قريبة أذهب ...

عندنا سبع حصص، ما عدا يوم الأربعاء حيث ...

أحياناً تكون الدروس الصعبة واحداً بعد الآخر، وهذا ... في أحيان أخرى تتنوع، ما يعطينا ...

على أية حال، فرصة الغداء تعطينا الراحة والطعام، وفيها ...

طبعاً، هذه الفرصة الطويلة تتميز بالكلام الذي لا فائدة فيه والضحك والتهريج (jesting) و ...

وهذا يذكرني بعمل قمت به أنا فخور به (proud of) دائماً، وهو أنني ساعدت طالباً في الصف الأصغر منا على التخلص من الضغط المتسلّط المؤذي (bullying)، فقد قمت ...

بعد أن وصلت إلى المدير، قام بالإشادة (praising) بي، طبعاً دون أن يذكر ...

أما العودة بعد المدرسة فتستغرق وقتاً أطول، لأنني وأصدقائي ...

In the above starters, the points of the task are attended not quite according to their sequence in the question. You can write about the points of the task in any order, but make sure that all points are included.

In such a task, some points might need to be assigned a longer portion of the piece, in which case you could write more or longer paragraphs for them.

You can see that the article suggested a starter for point e of the task, which is something that the student was proud of. This adds not only variety, but a more interesting thing that any reader would want to read to see what is going to be said.

Obviously, you can write about other details, such as a memorable event, an accident, a day that went in a different way and so on. Point e is optional – you don't have to add these other details, but writing about them can make up for any shortcomings in the rest of the points (in addition to the variety they add).

Try to use interesting openers (rather than the obvious ones) so as to tick your 'variety' box when the examiner corrects your paper. Bear in mind that variety is not confined to starting ideas, but can be applied to the piece as a whole – in vocabulary, grammar and the manner of your expression.

Don't overlook your punctuation and handwriting.

<u>Exercise 1</u> (a) Translate the sentence in bold: عندنا سبع حصص .

(b) Rewrite the sentence after changing حصص to دروس .

<u>Exercise 2</u> Why do think this student is so sarcastic about school as a whole? Write 130-150 words in response to his Facebook post (which seems to try to avoid any possible consequences), supporting it from personal experience or otherwise.

❖ After writing your articles, have them corrected by your teacher. Then rewrite them with the corrections and improvements, and keep them in your writing file.

> – لا أحب يوم الأربعاء لأنه يضيع عليّ المزيد من العلم بعد الظهر – الرياضة تضيع الوقت حسبما يقول أستاذ فلان. أؤيده في ذلك، لأن الرياضة متعبة...
>
> صحيح معظم الدروس صعبة بالنسبة إليّ، ولكن المصاعب هي التي تصنع الإنسان، كما تقول أستاذة فلانة...
>
> فرصة الغداء يجب أن تكون فرصة "غداء علم" كما يوجد "عشاء عمل" عند رجال الأعمال – نأكل ونحن نتحدث في الدروس، من أجل نيل الدرجات العالية التي توصلنا إلى الدراسة الجامعية العالية التي توصلنا إلى المهن التي فيها فلوس أكثر، وهذه تجعلنا نصرف على عوائلنا في المستقبل أكثر، في مدارس أفضل، حتى يحصلوا على الدرجات إلى آخر الدورة أعلاه...
>
> جيل بعد جيل يجري ويجري إلى ما لا نهاية...

رسمية-**19** في **130-150** كلمة، أكتب عن

(أ) الجمعيات/ النوادي والنشاطات خارج المدرسة

(ب) أي منها الذين شاركت أو لا تزال مشاركاً فيه

و (ت) لماذا.

FR-19 Write in 130-150 words on:

(a) the clubs and out-of-school activities that are available to you

(b) which of these you were or have been participating in

and (c) why.

Let's start here by drawing a mind-map containing the ideas, giving some details.

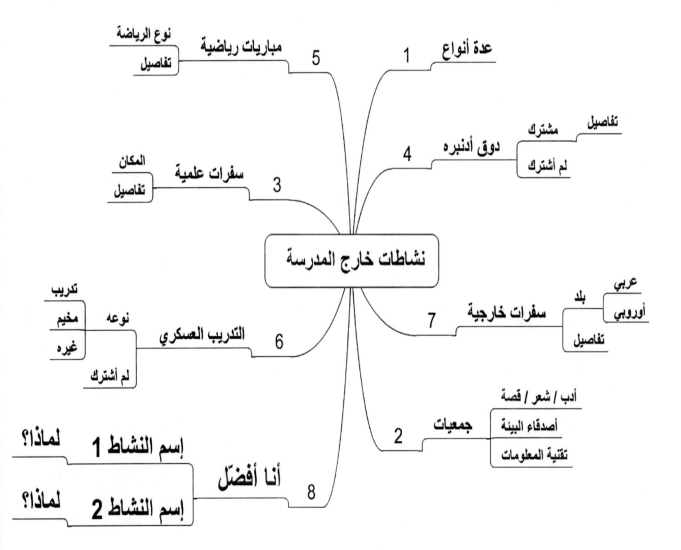

Use this mind-map to write the article. Note how you decide on the sequence after you have written the branches, by adding numbering to them.

Before using it, customize the map by crossing out the branches or sub-branches which are not valid, and also by adding the necessary details such as names of places or countries.

Next, decide how many words each of these branches needs. For such a mind-map with many branches (1-7) which are perhaps equally important, the number of words should probably be more or less equal. However, if you like a particular activity, or participate in it more than the rest, it is more likely that you will write about it more enthusiastically.

HOWEVER, much more should be written for branch 8 since it is the one concerning your explanation as to why you have chosen this or that activity; this is why, when you wrote your mind-map, you wrote that one larger so that you do not overlook this important aspect of your article. No less than a third of your article should be dedicated to branch 8, so that you have enough space to explain your choice.

You should try to avoid writing the above details as they are, in bullet points or similar. Instead, write them in paragraphs of balanced sizes, with good structure benefiting from varied grammatical forms and the use of connecting words. Pay attention also to your punctuation and handwriting.

Exercise The two photos relate to two of the activities mentioned in the mind-map above. Try to write 130-150 words, comparing the two activities, in both: their general type and the particulars of each, supporting your comparisons from personal experience or otherwise.

❖ After writing your articles, have them corrected by your teacher. Then rewrite them with the corrections and improvements, and keep them in your writing file.

رسمية-20 أكتب مقالة من 130-150 كلمة تبين فيها

(أ) المناسبات التي تقوم بها مدرستك (ب) هل تشترك فيها أم لا، ولماذ

(ت) هل تفضل مناسبات مدرسية أخرى، ولماذا.

FR-20 Write 130-150 words on (a) the events that your school holds, (b) whether you participate or not, and why, and (c) if you prefer other school events, and why.

من المؤسف أن مدرستنا لا تقوم بالكثير من المناسبات الكبيرة، <u>على أنّها</u> تشترك في مناسبات تقام في مدارس أخرى أو ملاعب تابعة لمدارس أو مؤسسات أخرى.

هناك مناسبة سنوية تحرص (make sure/is keen) مدرستنا على إقامتها، وهي الحفلة السنوية في آخر السنة. إشتركت في هذه المناسبة كل سنة، وفي شيء مختلف، أولاً لأني أحب أن أعطي ما أستطيع تقديمه، فإن الإنسان يجب أن يعطي ولا يأخذ فقط، وثانياً لأني أحب أن تنجح أي مناسبة تقيمها مدرستي، وهذه أهم مناسبة تُتَوِّج ('crowns') دراستنا ونشاطاتنا طيلة السنة.

يمكنني تقسيم المناسبات المدرسية إلى أنواع: علمية، ورياضية، وفنية، واجتماعية. بعض المدارس تهتم بنوع أو نوعين، <u>في حين</u> تهتم غيرها بجميعها. حفلة آخر السنة عندنا فيها عادةً فعّاليات (activities) علمية واجتماعية، وأحياناً فقرة أو فقرتان من الرياضة في الساحة دون حضور ولكن الزوار يطلعون عليها **أثناء** دخولهم.

أتمنى لو أن مدرستي اهتمت أكثر بالفنون كما تهتم مدرسة أختي أميرة، لأن العديد من طلابنا يحبون الفنون ويمتلكون الموهبة الفنية ودرس الرسم لا يكفي لإظهار (reveal) هذه المواهب، ويمكن أن يظهر فنان كبير إذا شاهد أعماله **المسؤولون** في التربية أو الأهالي الذين يزورون هكذا مناسبة، أو معرض تقيمه المدرسة، ممن يستطيعون مساعدته على التقدم، <u>وبعكسه</u> كيف سيُعرف؟   (184 كلمة)

<u>Exercise 1</u> Check how the piece above was successful in satisfying the requirements of the task. Use colour highlighting or another form of marking for quick future reference.

<u>Exercise 2</u> Translate the following <u>underlined words</u>: على أنّها ، في حين ، وبعكسه .

<u>Exercise 3</u> What is the grammar of the words in bold? أي ، أثناء ، المسؤولون

<u>Exercise 4</u> Write a similar article that relate to your own area, perhaps by first drawing a mind-map. You may use the same points and details as shown in the suggested piece above. Or better still, try to write your own discussion, ideas, opinions and suggestions.

❖ After writing your articles, have them corrected by your teacher. Then rewrite them with the corrections and improvements, and keep them in your writing file.

FUTURE ASPIRATIONS, STUDY AND WORK

رسمية-21 "التحدث بالعربية في بلدان لا تتحدث العربية ليس حملاً ثقيلاً، ولكنه رصيد يساعد على إيجاد وظيفة." أكتب حول هذا، في 130-150 كلمة، تبين فيها

(أ) هل تؤمن بهذه المقولة أم لا، ولماذا

(ب) هل تقوم بهذا على أية حال

(ت) إذا كنت تفعل، هل ساعدك هذا على إيجاد فرصة تدريب أو خبرة عمل.

تستطيع تناول القسم ت من السؤال من خلال خبرة شخص أو أشخاص تعرفهم وجدوا أن القيام بذلك (التحدث بالعربية) كان بالفعل رصيداً في الحصول على وظيفة بعد التخرج.

FR-21 'Speaking Arabic in non Arabic-speaking countries is not a disadvantage, but rather an asset to help find employment.' Write on this, in 130-150 words, explaining (a) whether you believe in this statement or not, and why, (b) whether you do speak Arabic anyway, and (c) if you do, how speaking Arabic has helped you in finding training or work experience. You can, instead, attend to c through the experience of people that you know who have found that speaking Arabic was indeed an asset in finding employment after graduation.

خالي لم يتوقف عن القول كلما التقى بنا: "هل تتحدثون بالعربية؟ اللغة الثانية لا سلاحَ مثلها!" لا أدري هل إنني مقتنعة بالمقولة لأنني أجدها صحيحة أم بسبب خالي!

أتصور أنها صحيحة، ولا سيما بعد انفتاح العالم على بعضه من خلال ثورة الاتصالات والمعلومات، فصار من الممكن التقديم على إعلان عمل يطلب اللغة العربية على الانترنت، وهناك آلاف المواقع للشركات. كما يمكن الحصول على عمل، أو حتى تدريب، في بلد عربي، وعندها سيكون الرصيد اللغوي مضاعفاً، أقصد أن معرفتي التامة باللغة الانجليزية ستعطي قوة لطلبي لأن الشركة ستجد أنها يمكن أن تستفيد مني، إن لم يكن الآن ففي المستقبل، في حال (if/in case) قامت بأعمال تجارية مع بريطانيا أو البلدان التي تتحدث الانجليزية اللغة الأكثر استخداماً في العالم.

وقد ساعدني هذا بالفعل، حيث سأقوم في الصيف بخبرة عمل في شركة سياحة في المغرب، وإن كان إلمامي (my command) باللغة الفرنسية التي ندرسها كلغة ثانية قد ساعد فيما أظن، لأن صاحب العمل (employer) سألني عنه في أكثر من إيميل.

عمي فؤاد يعمل في شركة لها مشاريع في البلدان العربية، وتمكّنه من اللغتين كان الرصيد الرئيسي وراء تعيينه (his employment). هو يقول هذا، فإنه **لم يكن ذا خبرة** (experience) عندما تقدم بالطلب.

لهذا، فإنني لن أتوقف عن استخدام اللغة العربية لأنها يمكن أن تدعم (supports) طلبات العمل التي سأقدمها (apply for) إلى وكالات التشغيل/التوظيف (employment agency) في المستقبل. المشكلة هي الأصدقاء الذين لا يحبون هذا، أيضاً أصدقاء مواقع التواصل الاجتماعي من العرب الذين يريدون التواصل بالانجليزية... ربما معهم حق، حيث يريدون هذا الرصيد هم أيضاً!   (229 كلمة)

Exercise 1 Study the piece above and check how successful it was in satisfying the requirements of the task by determining which paragraphs or sentences relate to which part of the task. Use colour highlighting or another form of marking for quick future reference (underlining was used to highlight connective words, fillers and useful words).

Exercise 2 What is the grammar of the sentence in bold? لم يكن ذا خبرة

Exercise 3 Translate the following underlined words: ولاسيما ، وعندها ، فيما أظن .

Exercise 4 How can the piece above be improved? Look into ways to make it more balanced:
 (xxxi) in terms of how much is written for each part of the task (you may omit, add or replace words, phrases or full sentences),
 (xxxii) using other, perhaps better, connective words or fillers,
 (xxxiii)   using other words or expressions that you think are better for the description and ideas given about this matter, which can be life-changing for many people.

Exercise 5 Try to condense this piece, to reduce it to around 130-150 words, while preserving the main points.

Exercise 6 Write (in around 130-150 words) a similar article, perhaps by first drawing a mind-map, and using, if you wish, similar ideas and detail to those in the suggested piece above, from your own experience, using your own discussion, ideas and opinions, and following a different sequence.

❖ After writing your articles, have them corrected by your teacher. Then rewrite them with the corrections and improvements, and keep them in your writing file.

رسمية-22 في 130-150 كلمة، إشرح لأخيك

(أ) كيف استفدت من الإرشاد المهني في المدرسة، بحيث يتضمن شرحك (ب) لماذا اقترُحت عليك هذه المهنة

أو تلك، و (ت) لماذا قررت أن تأخذ باتجاه معين، إن كنت توصّلت إلى هذا.

FR-22 (a) Explain, in 130-150 words, to your brother (a) how you have benefited from Careers Guidance at school, (b) including all the reasoning behind any advice you received, and (c) the direction you decided to pursue, if you did.

Let's start here by drawing a mind-map containing the ideas, giving some details.

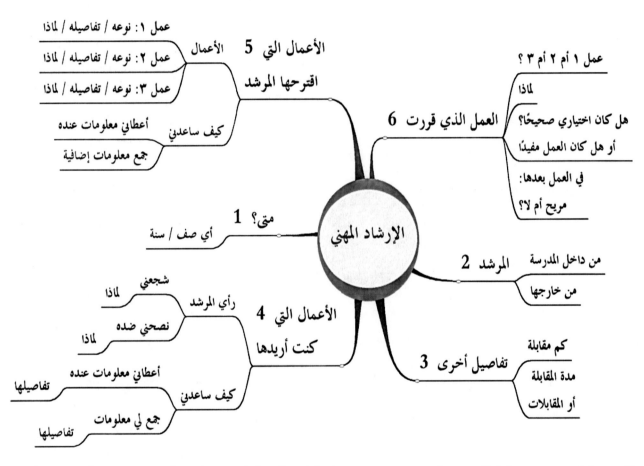

Use this mind-map to write the article. Decide how many words you think you need to write or can write about each of these branches, perhaps by seeing how many words each sub-branch needs. Not all of the sub-branches are to be used, since some are alternatives to others. At any rate, branches 4, 5 and 6 are the main ones for the task, with branches 4 and 5 forming the central part of the piece.

You should try to avoid writing the above details as they are, in bullet points or similar. Instead, write them in paragraphs of balanced sizes, with good structure benefiting from varied grammatical forms and the use of connecting words.

Pay attention also to your punctuation and handwriting.

❖ **After writing your article, have it corrected by your teacher. Then rewrite it with the corrections and improvements, and keep it in your writing file.**

رسمية-23 في 130-150 كلمة، أكتبي تقريرًا عن خبرة العمل التي قمت بها في الصيف.

بدأت التقرير بقولك: "إتفقت مع شركة تجارية على القيام بتدريب خبرة العمل عندهم ...". أذكري:

(أ) مدة التدريب (ب) نوع نشاط الشركة

(ت) الأعمال التي قمت بها والتعاون مع الموظفين

(ث) مبينة كيف كانت استفادتك من التدريب.

FR-23 Write, in 130-150 words, a report about the work experience which you did in the summer.

Imagine that you started the report by saying: 'I agreed with a commercial company to do my work experience with them ...' Address the following points:
(a) the training duration, (b) the field of activity of the company,
(c) the tasks you carried out, cooperation with their employees,
(d) explain how you benefited from the training.

إتفقت مع شركة تجارية على القيام بالتدريب لمدة أسبوعين في بداية شهر آب/ أغسطس، وذلك ضمن برنامج خبرة العمل للطلاب عندهم. تقوم الشركة بالاستيراد والتَّصدير (import and export)، حيث <u>تشتري بضائع من بريطانيا وتُصَدِّرها إلى الخارج أو تشتري من الخارج وتستوردها إلى بريطانيا.</u>

في الأسبوع الأول تدرّبت على أعمال السكرتارية: طباعة الرسائل على الحاسوب وترتيبها، واستلام الرسائل وإدخالها في الدفتر (log book)، والاختِزال (shorthand). وفي الأسبوع الثاني ركّزت على الأمور المالية كالإدخال والسّحْب من المصارِف (depositing and withdrawing from the banks)، وترتيب حسابات الشهر من المصاريف والخدمات (services, i.e. gas, electricity, cleaning etc).

قمت، خلال ذلك، بالأعمال الأخرى كإرسال البريد الإلكتروني والرّدّ على الهاتف واستلام البريد.

لم أشعر أن المدير كان مُرَحِّباً (welcoming/friendly) لأنه لم يكن يبتسم وكانت طلباته (his requests) كالأوامر (orders)، إلا أن السكرتيرة أخبرتني أن هذه طريقته كي يجعل المتدربّين (trainees) "لا يلعبون"! أما الموظّفون فكان بعضهم مُتَعاوناً بينما كان غيرهم أقلّ تعاوناً، ربما لأنهم كانوا مشغولين جداً ولم يكن عندهم وقت لتعليمي أو الصّبر على عملي البطيء أحياناً!

أثناء التدريب جاءت المدرسة المسؤولة عن خبرة العمل وقابلت المُشرف (supervisor) على تدريبي، الذي أكّد لها أنني أقوم بالتدريب بشكل جاد (in a serious manner) وأني تعلمت الكثير. كان فرحي عظيماً عندما قال الموظف: "لو في المستقبل قدّمَتْ للعمل عندنا فإننا سنوَظِّفُها (will employ me)".

بعد انتهاء التدريب كتبت الشركة شهادة (certificate) بتفاصيل الأعمال وكيف قمت بها بشكل جيد جداً. أهم منها أني حقّاً (indeed) تعلمت الكثير، فقد كنت أتعلم كل يوم شيئاً جديداً، كما تعلمت تَقَبُّل (accepting) النّقد (criticism)، الذي كان قاسياً أحياناً. كذلك عرفت كم يتعب أبي وأمي في العمل، وكم يتحمّلان من أجل توفير مصاريف المعيشة والدراسة والتسلية. (227 كلمة)

Exercise 1 Study the piece above and check how successful it was in satisfying the requirements of the task by determining which paragraphs or sentences relate to which part of the task. Use colour highlighting or another form of marking for quick future reference.

Exercise 2 Write the full grammar of the two sentences in bold:

. فكانَ بعضُهم مُتَعاوناً ، كانَ غيرُهم أقلَّ تعاوناً

Exercise 3 Translate the underlined sentences:

. تشتري بضائع من بريطانيا وتُصَدِّرها إلى الخارج أو تشتري من الخارج وتستوردِها إلى بريطانيا

Exercise 4 How can the piece above be improved? Look into ways to make it more balanced:

(xxxiv)   in terms of how much is written for each part of the task (you may omit, add or replace words, phrases or full sentences),

(xxxv) using other, perhaps better, connective words or fillers,

(xxxvi)   using other words or expressions that you think are better for the description and views given about that work experience training.

Exercise 5 Write (in around 130-150 words) a similar article, perhaps by first drawing a mind-map, and using, if you wish, similar ideas and detail to those in the suggested piece above, from your own experience, using your own discussion, ideas and opinions, and following a different sequence.

❖ After writing your articles, have them corrected by your teacher. Then rewrite them with the corrections and improvements, and keep them in your writing file.

رسمية-24 أكتب **130-150** كلمة حول العمل في المستقبل:

(أ) ما هي الأعمال التي تفكر فيها؟

(ب) ما رأيك بالأعمال الصغيرة ريثما تحصل على عمل تطمح إليه؟

(ت) هل عندك خطة للمستقبل تأخذ بالحُسبان الصعوبات المحتملة للتوظيف في البداية، وكيف هي؟

(ث) إدعم أجاباتك بالأسباب.

FR-24 Write 130-150 words on work in the future:
(a) What jobs you are thinking about?
(b) What is your opinion regarding doing small jobs while you are waiting for a job that you aspire to?
(c) Do have a future plan that takes into consideration the possible difficulties in employment from the start, and how?
(d) Support your answers with reasoning.

If you like, you can use some of the following paragraphs and sentences as starters or to give you ideas for writing this article.

حصل عندي تغيير مؤخّراً بخصوص العمل، حيث كنت أفكر في ...

إلا أنني الآن متحمس كثيراً للعمل في مجال ...

ذلك أنني أتصور أن هذا المجال سيكون ...

هذا يختلف عن الأعمال الصغيرة، مثل ...

فإني لا أفكر فيها، لأني أخشي أن ...

ولكني لن أعاند: خطتي المستقبلية تضمنت القبول ...

حيث أن المهم أن لا أجلس ...

يبدو/ يظهر أن هذا احتمال قوي، لأن ...

ولكن دعونا ننتظر، فمن يدري، الأمور تتغير ...

This task makes the justification of your ambitions and opinions a separate point – point d, not as part of each of points a,b and c. Thus you need to make sure that you do not overlook, by including it in your response to each of the three earlier points.

This advice is followed in the suggested opening statements. However, another reasonable way is to combine your response to points a and b in a single justification, since one can talk about the difference between small and 'good' jobs in the same time. Or, you can combine points b and c, say by incorporating possible available small jobs in your future plan. What is necessary is that all points are included.

Try to use interesting 'connective words' such as the words with wavy underlines used above to link the sentences in a way that flows, and at the same time to start another part of your description or explanation.

Don't overlook your punctuation and handwriting.

<u>Exercise 1</u> Translate the words with <u>dotted underlines</u>.

<u>Exercise 2</u> Suppose you have not thought about what kind of work you wish to do in the future and you come across this set of photos, indirectly describing these jobs and related professions - what would your thoughts and opinions be? Is it possible that they could start the process of thinking about this unescapable issue in your life? Write 130-150 words in response to this.

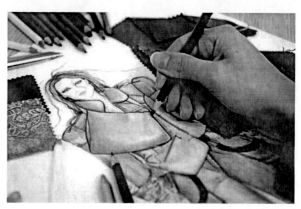

❖ **After writing your articles, have them corrected by your teacher. Then rewrite them with the corrections and improvements, and keep them in your writing file.**

INTERNATIONAL AND GLOBAL DIMENSION

رسمية-25 في 130-150 كلمة، أَكتب تقريراً موجَزاً

(أ) لترتيبات نشاط اجتماعي تساهم فيه في المدرسة أو النادي

(ب) محدّداً الواجبات المختلفة لكل فرد من المشتركين

(ت) موضحاً أسباب اختيارك لكل منهم.

FR-25 In 130-150 words, write a report summarizing

(a) the arrangements for a social event with an international element you are involved in at school or in a club,

(b) assigning the different tasks to specific individuals,

(c) justifying your choice in each case.

Let's start here by drawing a mind-map containing the ideas, and with some details.

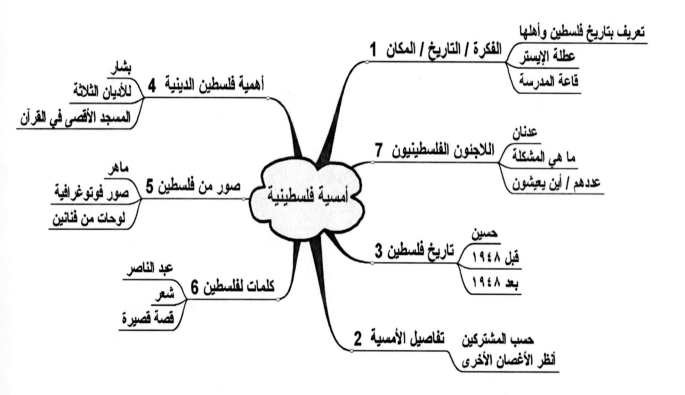

Use this mind-map to write the article. Decide how many words each of these branches needs. Here again, for such a mind-map with many branches which are perhaps equally important, the number of words should probably be more or less equal. Your writing about each point, however, should not be repetitive, i.e. Adnan did that... Husain did that ... You should try to introduce variety. The following suggested opening statements provide this kind of variety:

هذه السنة أردنا أن تكون الأمسية (evening) العربية **خاصة** بجزء عزيز (dear) من وطننا العربي: فلسطين. الفكرة...

قسّمنا العمل **بيننا** كالآتي: كان على حسين أن يجمع المعلومات عن تاريخ فلسطين ...

وبما أن أهمية فلسطين الدينية **موضوع مهم جداً** فقد قررنا أن يقوم بشار وحده بـ...

طبعًا كانت مسؤولية الصور من نَصيب (share) ماهر لأنه ...

أما شاعرنا الكبير (!) عبد الناصر فقد ...

أخيراً، من أحسن من عدنان، الذي عاش **لاجئاً** (refugee) في الأردن، من يعرف ويتحدث عن اللاجئين؟

You should try to avoid writing the above details as they are, in bullet points or similar. Instead, write them in paragraphs of balanced sizes, with good structure benefiting from varied grammatical forms and the use of connecting words. Pay attention also to your punctuation and handwriting.

Exercise1 Explain the grammar of each of the words in bold:

. لاجئاً ، موضوع مهم جداً ، بيننا ، خاصة

Exercise 2 Translate the underlined words: أردنا ، قسمنا ، قررنا .

Exercise 3 Write, in 130-150 words, a similar article, perhaps by first drawing a mind-map, on an event that you have participated in, or would like to participate in, that relates to a good cause. You may use the same points as shown in the suggested piece above. Or better still, try to create your own discussion, with your ideas, opinions and suggestions. You can find inspiration from the following good causes.

ذَوُو الاحتياجات الخاصّة people with special needs	المُحتاجون the needy
حقُوق الإنسان human rights	البيئة the environment

❖ After writing your articles, have them corrected by your teacher. Then rewrite them with the corrections and improvements, and keep them in your writing file.

رسمية-26 في 130-150 كلمة، أكتبي تقريراً موجزاً عما يلي:

(أ) هل سبق لك أن اتصلت، أو تودين الاتصال، بجمعية خيرية تعبرين عن رغبتك في العمل كمتطوعة معهم؟

(ب) كيف قمت، أو تقومين، بدعم طلبك ببيان الفوائد التي يمكن أن تتحقق من هذا العمل الطوعي، الآن أو في المستقبل؟

(ت) هل تضمن العمل الطوعي مناسبة لإحدى القضايا النبيلة، وإن لم يكن كذلك، كيف يمكن لمثل هذه المناسبة متعددة النشاطات أن تكون؟

FR-26 Write, in 130-150 words, a report, about the following:

(a) Have you contacted, or would like to contact, a charity to express your desire to work for them as a volunteer?

(b) How did you, or would you, support your request with reasons as to how useful such voluntary work would be to you now and in the future?

(c) Did your voluntary work involve a 'good cause' event that combined different activities, and if not, what would such a multi-activity event be like?

في السنة الماضية قامت طالبات مدرستنا بتنظيم واحدة من أجمل المناسبات الخيرية، جمعت فيها نشاطات علمية ورياضية وفنية واجتماعية. بدأت الفكرة عندما كتبت إيناس إلى جمعية مهتمة بالأطفال المصابين المرضى في بريطانيا تعرض (express/show) رغبتها في التطوع، وأن هذا التطوع سيشعرها بالراحة في مساعدة الآخرين، إضافة إلى أنه سيساعدها في تحقيق طموحها في المستقبل، وهو تأسيس (establishing) جماعة تربط بين جمعيات خيرية في بريطانيا وأخرى في البلاد العربية.

بعد العمل بضعة أسابيع، وبعد أن صارت مينا تذهب معها، قدمتا اقتراحاً إلى المدرسة لعمل مهرجان (carnival) خيري يستمر يومين بعنوان "أحب الخير في يومين!"

أقيم معرض فني مفتوح للزوار من الأهالي وسكنة المنطقة والمسؤولين في الهيئات التعليمية وطلبة من مدارس أخرى، استمر يومي السبت والأحد. بينما كانت حصة الرياضة يوم السبت من الصباح وحتى المساء، وبعض ألعاب الساحة والميدان جمعت مع ألعاب مسلّية فجمعت بين الرياضة والفكاهة.

صباح يوم الأحد تم إقامة المسابقة العلمية بين مدرستنا ومدرستين أخريتين كانتا قد قامتا بمسابقات مشابهة اشتركت مدرستنا في بعضها. فريق من كل مدرسة لقسم العلوم وآخر لقسم الرياضيات، وأسئلة لا تنتهي، أدارها مقدم برامج مسابقات في التلفزيون فزادها قوة.

ثم أخيراً المناسبة الاجتماعية مساء الأحد، جمعت الطالبات والأهالي وبعض المشتركين والحاضرين في اليومين الماضيين، وتم تقديم تمثيلية وموسيقى وقراءة شعر مع الطعام، وانتهى بتوزيع للجوائز.

ربما تسألون: أين "أحب الخير" إذاً؟!

إنه في التبرعات الكثيرة وفي رَيع (income) بيع اللوحات الفنية وبعض الأطعمة، أيضاً في الدعم (sponsorship) للمشاركات في مسابقات الرياضة ومسابقات العلوم من قبل الأهل والأصدقاء.

تم توزيع المبالغ بطريقة مناسبة إلى جمعيتين خيريتين، الأولى للطلاب الفقراء في دولة عربية، والثانية للجمعية البريطانية التي تطوعت فيها إيناس. (249 كلمة)

<u>Exercise 1</u> Study the piece above and check how successful it was in satisfying the requirements of the task by determining which paragraphs or sentences relate to which part of the task. Use colour highlighting or another form of marking for quick future reference.

<u>Exercise 2</u> Translate the following sentence in bold:

وبعض ألعاب الساحة والميدان جمعت مع ألعاب مسلّية فجمعت بين الرياضة والفكاهة .

<u>Exercise 3</u> Rewrite the following underlined words in their separate constituents then translate them: سيشعرها ، قدمتا ، أخريتين .

<u>Exercise 4</u> How can the piece above be improved? Look into ways to make it more balanced:

(xxxvii)   in terms of how much is written for each part of the task (you may omit, add or replace words, phrases or full sentences),

(xxxviii)   using other, perhaps better, connective words or fillers,

(xxxix)   using other words or expressions that you think are better for the description and ideas given about that charity event.

<u>Exercise 5</u> Try to condense this piece, to reduce it to around 130-150 words, while preserving the main points.

<u>Exercise 6</u> Write (in around 130-150 words) a similar article, perhaps by first drawing a mind-map, and using, if you wish, similar ideas and detail to those in the suggested piece above, from your own experience, using your own discussion, ideas, opinions and suggestions, and following a different sequence.

❖ After writing your articles, have them corrected by your teacher. Then rewrite them with the corrections and improvements, and keep them in your writing file.

رسمية-27 "إدفع أكثر واشتر الأخضر، أم لماذا أفعل هذا؟!"

أكتب 130-150 كلمة حول هذا الموضوع من خلال الإجابة على ما يلي:

(أ) هل تعتقد أن القضايا "الخضراء" مهمة، ولماذا؟

(ب) في أي جانب من جانبي المسألة أنت تقف، ولماذا؟

(ت) كيف تصف الشخص "الأخضر"؟

(ث) إذا قررت أن تصبح "أخضر" ما هو الشيء الأكثر أهمية الذي ستغيره في حياتك؟

FR-27 'Pay more and buy green, or why should I?!'

Write 130-150 words on this issue, answering the following questions:

(a) Do you think that 'green' issues are important, and why?

(b) On which side of the argument do you stand, and why?

(c) How do you describe a 'green person'?

(d) If you go 'green', what is the single most important thing you are going to change in your life?

If you like, you can use some of the following paragraphs and sentences as starters or to give you ideas for writing this article.

كيف لا تكون مهمة وهي تتعلق بـ ...

أكثر من هذا، إن القضايا الخضراء تعني – وببساطة – ...

طبعاً أقف في جانب الاهتمام بكل ...

بل أستطيع القول أنني، ومنذ بضع سنوات، ...

فإنني أستطيع وصف نفسي كشخص "أخضر"، فأعرف ...

بالإضافة إلى ذلك، الشخص الأخضر هو الذي ...

إن أهم شيء في المعيشة الخضراء هو القيام ...

ولكن يمكن أن يجد البعض أن الأهم منه هو ...

على أية حال، التغيير نحو "الأخضر" هو التغيير نحو "الأحسن"!

In the above starters, the points of the task are attended to according to their sequence in the question. Although this is a reasonable, straightforward approach, you can write about the points of the task in any order. But make sure that all points are included.

In addition, you can see that there are two starting statements for every point of the task. This again is a reasonable way to make your piece balanced. That said, some points might need to be assigned a longer portion of the piece, in which case you could write more or longer paragraphs for them.

Try to use interesting openers so that to tick your 'variety' box when the examiner corrects your paper. In the above suggestions, you can see the strong start that tells you from the outset how enthusiastic the writer is about this issue. Obviously, one can write with a softer approach so that the reader doesn't think that the writer is a fanatic that is treating this issue from a relatively emotional standpoint. Both are absolutely fine.

Don't overlook your punctuation and handwriting.

Exercise 1 Translate the words with <u>double underlines</u>.

Exercise 2 For the following sentences and clauses:

, أستطيع القول ، أستطيع وصف ، هو القيام ، هو التغيير

(a) What is the grammatical derivation that combines the underlined words?

(b) Write the underlined words in verbal expression.

Exercise 3 'Going green means going white for air, and going blue for water, and going all colours for all plants and animals.' Do you think that using the colour 'green' might only have made people's concerns about these vital matters more marginalised? How? Write 130-150 words about this viewpoint.

المعيشة الخضراء =

المعيشة البيضاء من أجل الهواء + المعيشة الزرقاء من أجل الماء + المعيشة الملونة من أجل النباتات والحيوانات

وإلا فلم نصنع شيئاً كثيراً!

❖ After writing your articles, have them corrected by your teacher. Then rewrite them with the corrections and improvements, and keep them in your writing file.

رسمية-28 في 130-150 كلمة أكتبي حول "حماية المصادر الطبيعية لكوكب الأرض"، متناولةً:

(أ) حسب رأيك، ما أهم مصدر طبيعي يجب حمايته، ولماذا؟

(ب) هل هناك معلومات اطلعت عليها حول المخاطر المحيطة بهذا المصدر، مع مثال منها؟

(ت) كيف يمكن للمجتمع أن يقوم بخطوات عملية لحماية المصدر الطبيعي؟

(ث) وكيف يمكنك القيام بخطوات عملية في حياتك اليومية؟

FR-28 In 130-150 words, write on 'protecting planet Earth's natural resources':
(a) In your opinion, what is the most important natural resource that needs protection, and why?
(b) What information do you have on the dangers threatening this resource, with an example?
(c) What practical steps can society take to protect this natural resource?
(d) And what practical steps can you take in this regard in your daily life?

لا حياة ممكنة دون ماء، فهو أهم مصدر طبيعي على الأرض. جميع الكائنات الحية تحتاج إليه، جميع الصناعات – ومنها الغذاء والدواء – تحتاج إليه، وطبعاً الزراعة.

بالرغم من أن الماء يغطي ثلاثة أرباع سطح الأرض فإنه الآن مهدّد (threatened)! حقاً إنه شيء لا يصدق، ولكنها الحقيقة. فطبقاً لمنظمة الصحة العالمية (according to the WHO) **لا تتوفر المياه النظيفة لنصف سكان العالم**، ولا يتوفر الماء الصالح للشرب لمليار إنسان! ويموت آلاف الأطفال يومياً بسبب أمراض تنتج من تلوث مياه الشرب. أرقام مخيفة حقاً.

إذاً، الماء أهم مصدر طبيعي يجب حمايته، ودون تأخير.

هناك مخاطر عديدة تهدد الماء تهديداً شديداً، أهمها زيادة الطلب، بسبب الزيادة المستمرة في عدد السكان، والتلوث الكبير من المصانع، والزراعة التي تستخدم الكيمياويات، ورمي النفايات في الأنهار والبحار. وستؤدي زيادة الاستهلاك (consumption) إلى نقص في موارد المياه، وهذا سيرفع أسعار الغذاء. وسيؤدي أيضاً إلى التأثير على الزراعة، فيقل الإنتاج، فيتعرض مئات الملايين لخطر الموت جوعاً.

من الخطوات العملية تغيير طريقة ريّ (irrigation) المزارع، والاقتصاد في استهلاك المصانع، بحيث تتم مراقبة هدر (waste) المياه فيها. كما يمكن الاقتصاد في غسل الشوارع والأشجار باتباع طرق حديثة.

وأتصور أن طرق توليد الكهرباء التي لا تستخدم الماء (كالهواء والطاقة الشمسية) ستساعد. وربما يساعد التدوير (recycling) في تقليل الاستهلاك في إنتاج الملابس والغذاء وغيرها.

أما الخطوات العملية التي أقوم بها فعلاً، فإني أراقب عدم ترك حنفية المغسلة أو الحمام مفتوحة أثناء الغسل. وأشجع أهلي على الاقتصاد ــ مثلاً عدم غسل السيارة دون حاجة، وعدم سقي الحديقة دون داع، والاستفادة من ماء المطر الذي نجمعه في حاوية في سقي الورد.

فلا تتوقفوا عن القيام بهذه الخطوات، خدمةً للأرض ولمن يعيش عليها. (247 كلمة)

Exercise 1 Study the piece above and check how successful it was in satisfying the requirements of the task by determining which paragraphs or sentences relate to which part of the task. Use colour highlighting or another form of marking for quick future reference.

Exercise 2 Name the grammatical topic that relate to each of the three لا in the clause

and sentences in bold, and what each of them does: لا حياة، لا تتوفر، لا تتوقفوا .

Exercise 3 Name the different grammatical positions of the three underlined accusative words: تهديداً، جوعاً، خدمةً.

Exercise 4 How can the piece above be improved? Look into ways to make it more balanced:

(xl) in terms of how much is written for each part of the task (you may omit, add or replace words, phrases or full sentences),

(xli) using other, perhaps better, connective words or fillers,

(xlii) using other words or expressions that you think are better for the information given about this extremely important issue.

Exercise 5 Write (in around 130-150 words) a similar article, perhaps by first drawing a mind-map, and using, if you wish, similar ideas and detail to those in the suggested piece above, from your own experience, using your own discussion, ideas, opinions and suggestions, and following a different sequence.

❖ After writing your articles, have them corrected by your teacher. Then rewrite them with the corrections and improvements, and keep them in your writing file.

ثبت بقطع الكتابة

INDEX
for the Written Pieces

الملاحق

ملحق 1 قائمة المفردات

Appendix 1 Vocabulary

If you are following a particular syllabus such as the Edexcel GCSE Specification, you will find a long list of vocabulary, split in two general categories: high-frequency words and topic-related words, with each category containing vocabulary that relate to the different topics in the Specification. This vocabulary can be used by examiners, which means that candidates should have a good knowledge of it.

Students should do their best to learn as much vocabulary as possible as this is the substance of the language, any language, and the aim is to use the language, not merely sit examinations. Also, students should become used to analysing the complex words that are often formed in Arabic by merging nouns and pronouns, verbs and pronouns, nouns or verbs with preposition etc. Obviously, this should not become a burden, rather a simple, quick look into the structure of words (and sentences for that matter) so as to determine the vocabulary involved in such words.

In this edition

Since the vocabulary list is <u>now available, with full translation, for free download, in both Word format and pdf, from Edexcel's website, there is no point in including it in this Guide</u>:

- Vocabulary list from pages 75-197
- Website link

<u>http://qualifications.pearson.com/en/qualifications/edexcel-gcses/arabic-2017.coursematerials.html#filterQuery=category:Pearson-UK:Category%2FSpecification-and-sample-assessments</u>

You might find it useful to make a hard copy of these lists to have them at hand when you are studying – i.e. when you are reading the written pieces or writing the pieces requested in the exercises.

Please note that since the written pieces use words other than those in these lists, users may need to consult a dictionary, should they want to check the meaning of such words.

ملحق 2 جداول الأفعال

Appendix 2 Verb Tables

ملاحظة: نوع الفعل بين القوسين في العمود الأول يتعلق بالتصريف، حتى ولو كان جذره الثلاثي من نوع آخر، لأن المهم هو الفعل أدناه (من إحدى الصيغ العشر للجذر الثلاثي).

مثلاً: الفعل "إتَّصَلَ" جذره الثلاثي (الصيغة الأولى للفعل) هو "وَصَلَ" أي أنه من نوع "المثال"، ولكنه هنا بصيغة "إفتعل = إ و ت ص ل (قلبت الواو تاء للتسهيل، فصار إتّصلَ وليس إوتصل)، وهذه الصيغة "إفتعل" يتم تصريفها كالفعل السالم. لهذا كتبنا (مثل السالم). وهكذا.

تمرين – ملء جداول الأفعال:

تحتوي جداول الأفعال على إسناد الأفعال (المتكلم والمخاطب والغائب، للماضي والمضارع والأمر) لمختلف الأفعال المهمة في هذا المستوى الدراسي، مع ترك كل فعل كان الفعل المشابه له قد تم ملء إسناده قبله في الجدول – مع الإشارة إلى هذا تحته. هذا من شأنه تشجيع الطلاب على إكمال الجداول كنوع من التمرين الذي يساعد في دراسة هذا الموضوع.

Exercise - completing the verb tables:

The table includes conjugation (1st, 2nd and 3rd person, in the past, present and the imperative tenses) of the different types of verbs that are common for this level, but leaving blank every verb where the same type has already been completed earlier - indicating this under it. This is to encourage students to complete the table themselves as a kind of exercise that should help in studying these conjugations.

أمر (-/مُخاطَب/-) - أنتَ أنتِ أنتُما أنتُم أنتُنَّ -	مضارع (متكلّم/مُخاطَب/غائب) أنا نحنُ أنتَ أنتِ أنتُما أنتُم أنتُنَّ هُوَ هِيَ هُما هُما هُم هُنَّ	ماضٍ (متكلّم/مُخاطَب/غائب) أنا نحنُ أنتَ أنتِ أنتُما أنتُم أنتُنَّ هُوَ هِيَ هُما هُما هُم هُنَّ	الفعل
إتصلْ إتصلي إتصلا إتصلوا إتصلْنَ	أتصلُ نتصلُ تتصلُ تتصلين تتصلان تتصلون تتصلنّ يتصلُ تتصلُ يتصلان تتصلان يتصلون يتصلْنَ	إتصلتُ إتصلنا إتصلتَ إتصلتِ إتصلتما إتصلتم إتصلتنّ إتصل إتصلتْ إتصلا إتصلتا إتصلوا إتصلْنَ	إتَّصَلَ to call/ring (مثل السالم)
			أجابَ to answer (أجوف)
أحِبَّ أحِبّي أحِبّا أحِبّوا أحْبِبْنَ -	أُحِبُّ نُحِبُّ تُحِبُّ تُحِبّينَ تُحِبّان تُحِبّون تُحْبِبْنَ يُحِبُّ تُحِبُّ يُحِبّان تُحِبّان يُحِبّون يُحْبِبْنَ	أحببتُ أحببنا أحببتَ أحببتِ أحببتُما أحببتم أحببتنَّ أحَبَّ أحَبَّتْ أحَبّا أحَبَّتا أحبُّوا أحْبَبْنَ	أحَبَّ to love (مُضعَّف)

			أَحَسَّ to feel (مُضَعَّف) مثل "أحبَّ"
			إحمَرَّ to become red (مضعف) مثل "أحبَّ"
- إختَر إختاري إختارا إختاروا إخترنَ -	أختارُ نَختارُ تَختار تختارين تختاران تختارون تخترنَ يختار تختار يختاران تختاران يختارون يخترنَ	إخترتُ إخترنا إخترتَ إخترتِ إخترتُما إخترتُم إخترتُنَّ إختارَ إختارتْ إختارا إختارتا إختاروا إخترنَ	إختارَ to choose (أجوف)
- خُذْ خُذي خُذا خُذوا خُذنَ -	أأخذُ/آخذُ نأخذُ تأخذ تأخذين تأخذان تأخذون تأخذنَ يأخذ تأخذ يأخذان تأخذان يأخذون يأخذنَ	أخذتُ أخذنا أخذتَ أخذتِ أخذتُما أخذتُم أخذتُنَّ أخذ أخذتْ أخذا أخذتا أخذوا أخذنَ	أخَذَ to take (مهموز)
- أخِّرْ أخِّري أخِّرا أخِّروا أخِّرنَ -	أوَخِّرُ نُوَخِّرُ تؤَخِّر تؤَخِّرين تؤَخِّران تؤَخِّرون تؤَخِّرنَ يؤَخِّر تؤَخِّر يؤَخِّران تؤَخِّران يؤَخِّرون يؤَخِّرنَ	أخَّرتُ أخَّرنا أخَّرتَ أخَّرتِ أخَّرتُما أخَّرتُم أخَّرتُنَّ أخَّر أخَّرتْ أخَّرا أخَّرتا أخَّروا أخَّرنَ	أخَّرَ to delay (سالِم)
- أدِرْ أديري أديرا أديروا أدِرنَ -	أديرُ نُديرُ تدير تديرين تديران تديرون تُدِرنَ يديرُ تدير يديران تديران يديرُون يدِرنَ	أدَرتُ أدَرنا أدَرتَ أدَرتِ أدَرتُما أدَرتُم أدَرتُنَّ أدار أدارتْ أدارا أدارتا أداروا أدَرنَ	أدارَ to turn (a thing) (أجوف)
			أرادَ to want (أجوف) "مثل أدار"
			أرسَلَ to send (سالِم) مثل "إتّصلَ"
			إستَدارَ to turn (أجوَف) "مثل أدار"
			إستَطاعَ to be able to (أجوف) "مثل أدار"

			إسْتَمَرَّ to continue (مضعف) مثل "أحبَّ"
			إسْتَمَعَ to listen (سالِم) مثل "إتَّصلَ"
			إسْتَيْقَظَ to wake up (سالِم) مثل "إتَّصلَ"
إشتَرِ إشتَري إشترِيا إشتَروا إشترينَ -	أشتري نَشتري تشتري تشترين تشتريان تشترون تشترينَ يشتري تشتري يشتريان تشتريان يشترون يشترينَ	إشترَيْتُ إشترَيْنا إشترَيْتَ إشترَيْتِ إشترَيْتُما إشترَيْتُم إشترَيْتُنَّ إشترى إشترَتْ إشترَيا إشترَتا إشترَوا إشترَيْنَ	إشْتَرى to buy (ناقص)
			إعتَقَدَ to believe in (سالِم) مثل "إتَّصلَ"
			أكَلَ to eat (مهموز) مثل "أخذ"
آمِنْ آمِني آمِنا آمِنوا آمِنَّ -	أُؤْمِنُ نُؤمِنُ تُؤمِن تُؤمنين تُؤمنان تُؤمنون تُؤمنَّ يُؤمِن تُؤمِن يُؤمنان تُؤمنان يُؤمنون يُؤمِنَّ	آمَنْتُ آمَنّا آمَنْتَ آمَنْتِ آمَنْتُما آمَنْتُم آمَنْتُنَّ آمَنَ آمَنَتْ آمَنا آمَنَتا آمَنوا آمَنَّ	آمَنَ to believe in (مهموز)
			إنتَظَرَ to wait (سالِم) مثل "إتَّصلَ"
			إنْتَهى to end (ناقص) مثل "إشترى"

الأمر	المضارع	الماضي	الفعل
- أنهِ أنهي أنهيا أنهوا أنهينَ -	أنهي نُنهي تُنهي تُنهين تُنهيان تُنهون تُنهينَ يُنهي تُنهي يُنهيان تُنهون يُنهينَ	أنهيْتُ أنهيْنا أنهيْتَ أنهيْتِ أنهيْتُما أنهيتُم أنهيتُنَّ أنهى أنهتْ أنهيا أنهَيتا أنهوا أنهيْنَ	أنهى to finish (ناقص)
صِلْ صِلي صِلا صِلوا أوصِلْنَ	أوصِلُ نُوصِلُ تُوصِلُ توصِلين توصلان توصلون توصِلْنَ يوصِلُ توصِلُ يوصلان توصلان يوصلون يوصِلْنَ	أوصَلْتُ أوصَلْنا أوصَلْتَ أوصَلْتِ أوصَلْتما أوصَلْتم أوصَلْتنَّ أوصَلَ أوصَلْت أوصَلا أوصَلَتا أوصَلوا أوصَلْنَ	أوصَلَ to connect (مثال)
بِعْ بيعي بيعا بيعوا بِعْنَ	أبيعُ نَبيعُ تَبيعُ تَبيعين تَبيعان تَبيعون تَبِعْنَ يَبيعُ تبيعُ يبيعان تبيعان يبيعون يبِعْنَ	بعْتُ بِعْنا بعْتَ بعْتِ بعْتُما بعْتم بعْتُنَّ باع باعَت باعا باعَتا باعُوا بِعْنَ	باعَ to sell (أجوف)
			بَحَثَ to search (سالِم) مثل "إتّصلَ"
			بَعَثَ to send (سالِم) مثل "إتّصلَ"
إبْكِ إبْكي إبْكيا إبْكوا إبْكينَ	أبْكي نَبْكي تَبْكي تَبْكين تَبْكيان تَبْكون تَبْكينَ يَبْكي تَبْكي تبْكيان تبْكيان يبْكون يبْكينَ	بكَيْتُ بكَيْنا بكَيْتَ بكَيْتِ بكَيْتُما بكَيْتُم بكَيْتُنَّ بكى بكَث بكَيا بكَيتا بكَوا بكَيْنَ	بكى to cry (ناقص)
			تَحَدَّثَ to talk (سالِم) مثل "إتّصلَ"
			تَرَكَ to leave / abandon (سالِم) مثل "إتّصلَ"
			جاءَ to come (أجوف) مثل "باع"
			جاعَ to become hungry (أجوف) مثل "باع"

			حاوَلَ to try (سالم) مثل "إتّصلَ"
			حَضَر to come (سالم) مثل "إتّصلَ"
			حَضَّرَ to prepare (سالِم) مثل "إتّصلَ"
			خَرَجَ to go out (سالِم) مثل "إتّصلَ"
			خَسِرَ to lose (سالِم) مثل "إتّصلَ"
			دَخَّنَ to smoke (سالِم) مثل "إتّصلَ"
			دَردَشَ to chat (سالِم) مثل "إتّصلَ"
			دعى to invite (ناقص) مثل "بكى"

			ذَهَبَ to go (سالم) مثل "إتّصلَ"
	أرى نَرَى تَرى تَرَين تَريان تَرون تَرَيْنَ يَرى تَرى يَرَيان تَريان يَرَون يَرَيْنَ	رأيْتُ رأينا رأيْتَ رأيْتِ رأيْتُما رأيْتُم رأيْتُنَّ رأى رأتْ رأيا رأيتا رأوا رأيْنَ	رَأى to see (مهموز ناقص)
			رَبَطَ to connect (سالم) مثل "إتّصلَ"
			رَمى to throw (ناقص) مثل "بكى"
			زارَ to visit (أجوف) مثل "باع"
			سافَرَ to travel (سالم) مثل "إتّصلَ"
إسْألْ إسْألِي إسْألا إسْألا إسْألوا إسْألْنَ	أسْألُ نَسْألُ تَسْألُ تَسْألين تَسْألان تَسْألون تَسْألْنَ يسْألُ تَسْألُ يسْألان تَسْألان يسْألُون يسْألْنَ	سألْتُ سألْنا سألْتَ سألْتِ سألْتما سألْتم سألْتنَّ سألَ سألتْ سألا سألتا سألوا سألْنَ	سَألَ to ask (مهموز)
			ساقَ to drive (أجوف) مثل "باع"
			سَقَطَ to fall (سالم) مثل "إتّصلَ"

			شاهَدَ to watch (سالِم) مثل "إتّصلَ"
			شَرِبَ to drink (سالِم) مثل "إتّصلَ"
			شَعَرَ to feel (سالِم) مثل "إتّصلَ"
			صاحَ to cry (أجوف) مثل "باع"
			صادَ to hunt (أجوف) مثل "باع"
			ضاعَ to get lost (أجوف) مثل "باع"
			ضَحِكَ to laugh (سالِم) مثل "إتّصلَ"
			ضَرَبَ to hit/beat (سالِم) مثل "إتّصلَ"

			طَلَبَ to request (سالِم) مثل "إتّصلَ"
			عاشَ to live (أجوف) مثل "باع"
			عَرَفَ to know (سالِم) مثل "إتّصلَ"
			عَلِمَ to know (سالِم) مثل "إتّصلَ"
			عَمِلَ to work (سالِم) مثل "إتّصلَ"
			غابَ to be absent (أجوف) مثل "باع"
			غادَرَ to leave (سالِم) مثل "إتّصلَ"
			فازَ to win (أجوف) مثل "باع"

			فَتَحَ to open (سالِم) مثل "إتّصلَ"
			فَضَّلَ to prefer (سالِم) مثل "إتّصلَ"
			فَكَّرَ to think (سالِم) مثل "إتّصلَ"
			قادَ to lead (أجوف) مثل "باع"
إقرَأ إقرئي إقرءا إقرءوا (إقرؤوا) إقرأنَ	أقرَأ نَقرَأ تَقرَأ تَقرَئين تَقرَءان تَقرَؤون (تقرؤون) تَقرَأنَ يقرَأ تَقرَأ يقرَءان تَقرَءان يقرَؤون (يقرؤون) يقرَأنَ	قَرَأتُ قَرَأنا قَرَأتَ قَرَأتِ قَرَأتُما قَرَأتم قَرَأتنَ قَرَأ قَرَأتْ قَرَءا قَرَأتا قَرَأوا (قرؤوا) قَرَأنَ	قالَ to say (أجوف) مثل "باع"
			قامَ to stand up (أجوف) مثل "باع"
			قَرَأ to read (مهموز)
			قَرَّرَ to decide (سالِم) مثل "إتّصلَ"
			كانَ to be (أجوف) مثل "باع"

			كَتَبَ to write (سالِم) مثل "إتّصلَ"
			لاحَظَ to notice (سالِم) مثل "إتّصلَ"
			لَبِسَ to wear (سالِم) مثل "إتّصلَ"
			لَعِبَ to play (سالِم) مثل "إتّصلَ"
			مَشى to walk (ناقص) مثل "بكى"
			لَبِسَ to wear (سالِم) مثل "إتّصلَ"
			نامَ to sleep (أجوف) مثل "باع"
			نَجَحَ to succeed / pass (سالِم) مثل "إتّصلَ"

			نَزَلَ to go down (سالِم) مثل "إتّصلَ"
			نَزَّلَ to download (سالِم) مثل "إتّصلَ"
			نَظَرَ to see (سالِم) مثل "إتّصلَ"
			هَجَمَ to attack (سالِم) مثل "إتّصلَ"
			وَجَدَ to find (مثال)
			وَجَبَ must (مثال) مثل "وجد"
			وَصَلَ to arrive (مثال) مثل "وجد"
			وَضَعَ to put / lay down (مثال) مثل "وجد"

ملحق 3 أخطاء شائعة

Appendix 3 Common Mistakes

الموضوع	الصَّواب	الخَطأ
pronunciation	أيضًا	ظ / ض - أيظًا
words ending in *tenween*	خاصةً / أيضًا	خاصتًا / أيضاً / أيضن
words ending in *ta' meftoohah* ت	لا زالت موجودة	ت / ة - لا زالة موجودة
words ending in *ta' merbooteh* ة	رية بيت	ت / ة - ريت بيت
words ending in *alif meqsooreh*	... أخرى	غرفة أخرة
verbs ending in *alif meqsooreh*	أتمنى / ... يتلقى	أتمنا / أرجو أن يتلق
words ending in *ha'*	لأنه / هذه / له / فيه / تساعده	لأنة / هذة / لة / فية / تساعدة
adding pronouns	لأنها	لئن هي
general spelling	في رأيي / ضد / منذ / الرياضة	في رأي / ضض / من ذو / أرياضة
joining of ف / ك	فأنا / فهناك / فيمكن / فالحرب / كالتاريخ	فا أنا / فاهناك / فا يمكن / فلحرب / كل تاريخ
joining of ل + ال	للجنة / للظروف / للطلاب / للناس	لللاجنة / لظروف / لا الطلاب / لا لناس
joining of بـ + ال	بالنسبة / باللغة / بل بالعكس	بنسبة / بللغة / بلبا لعكس

joining of في + ال	في اليوم / في العالم	فل يوم / فالعالم
joining of ل + أن	لأن / لأنها / لأنا - لأننا	لئن / لئن هي / لئن اننا
joining of إن / أن	... أن نقول / إن شاء الله	يمكن النقول / إنشاء الله
relative pronoun	... الذين يدرسون / ... التي تقودها / الذي يراد ...	الطلاب اليدرسون اللغة / السيارات التقودها الرجال / اليراد المشاركة
present tense plural endings (when not preceded by أداة نصب or أداة جزم)	... يسافرون / ... يسافرون	الأولاد يسافروا / عندما يسافروا
joining سwith *hemzated* verb	سأعطيها / سآخذ	سؤعطيها / سأأخذ
masculine and feminine	الإعلام هو الوسيلة	الإعلام هي الوسيلة
كان and its sisters (determining its إسم and خبر ; the former may come after the later)	أصبح للإعلام دور كبير	أصبح للإعلام دوراً كبيراً
إنّ and its sisters (determining its إسم and خبر ; the former may come after the later)	إن للإعلام دوراً كبيراً	إن للإعلام دور كبير
idafeh	إيجاد حل، عمل / غير المتوقعة، المقصودة	إيجاد حلاً، عملاً / الغير متوقعة، مقصودة
using feminine for non-humans	هذه الألعاب	هؤلاء الألعاب
tense after إذا	إذا كانت الرحلة مفتوحة ...	إذا الرحلة مفتوحة لكل الأعمار
use of إلاّ	إلا من نفس العائلة	إلى من نفس العائلة